images
stone
b.c.

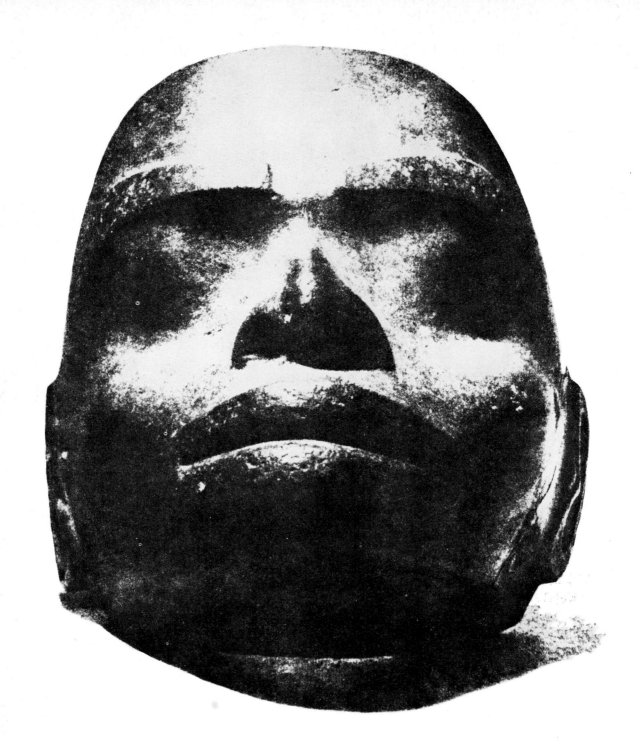

images
stone
b.c.

WILSON DUFF

THIRTY CENTURIES OF
NORTHWEST COAST INDIAN SCULPTURE

Photographs and Drawings by Hilary Stewart

n exhibition originating at the Art Gallery of Greater Victoria, Richard Simmins, Director

HANCOCK HOUSE PUBLISHERS

ISBN Cloth 0-919654-27-4
ISBN Soft 0-919654-29-0

Designed by Nicholas Newbeck Design.
Type set in Palatino by White Computer Typesetting.
Printed in Canada by The Bryant Press Limited.

This book was originally prepared and
published in Canada in 1975 by

Hancock House Publishers, Ltd.

3215 Island View Road, Saanichton, British Columbia, Canada.

The publisher wishes to acknowledge the kind assistance of the
Canada Council in supporting this project.

HANCOCK HOUSE PUBLISHERS, LTD.

Art Gallery of Greater Victoria
March 4, 1975 to April 13, 1975

Vancouver Art Gallery
May 7, 1975 to June 4, 1975

Royal Ontario Museum, Toronto
June 23, 1975 to August 24, 1975

National Museum of Man, Ottawa
November 15 , 1975 to January 11 , 1976

Winnipeg Art Gallery
January 27, 1976 to March 7 , 1976

Lenders to the Exhibition

Dr. C. E. Borden, Vancouver

British Columbia Provincial Museum, Victoria

Cariboo College, Kamloops

Centennial Museum, Vancouver

Mrs. W. H. Cross, Sidney

Mr. & Mrs. R. E. B. Gore-Langton, Victoria

Mr. John Hauberg, Seattle

Ms. Dolly Jensen, Ketchikan

Kamloops Museum, Kamloops

Langley Centennial Museum, Fort Langley

Lillooet Museum, Lillooet

McCord Museum of McGill University, Montreal

Mission District Historical Society, Mission City

Musée de l'Homme, Paris

Museum of Anthropology, University of British Columbia,
Vancouver

Museum of Archaeology and Anthropology,
Simon Fraser University, Burnaby

Museum of Northern British Columbia, Prince Rupert

Museum of the American Indian, Heye Foundation, New York

Philadelphia Museum of Art, Philadelphia

Mr. W. R. Quanstrom, Terrace

Mr. Barry Roome, Shawnigan Lake

Smithsonian Institution, Washington

The National Museum of Man, Ottawa

Vernon Board of Museum, Archives and Art Gallery, Vernon

contents

foreword

Richard Simmins

IMAGES: STONE: B.C. is truly a co-operative venture which involved scholars and museum officials in Canada, the United States and France.

I am especially indebted to J. D. Herbert, director of the Vancouver Museums and Planetarium, whose initial support of the project enabled me to apply for and receive generous funding for a unique exhibition. Herbert also placed the facilities of the Centennial Museum at our disposal, including the services of Roy Waterman who made casts from objects loaned by the British Columbia Provincial Museum and the Museum of Anthropology of the University of British Columbia. Dr. Frederick J. Dockstader of the Museum of the American Indian, Heye Foundation, New York, was especially gracious in permitting fourteen stone sculptures to leave the museum during a particularly difficult period. While little material remains in private hands, individual collectors, as noted in the catalogue, assisted without reservation, although the extended tour made for extraordinary inconvenience. The bringing together of the twin stone masks from The National Museum of Man in Ottawa and the Musée de l'Homme in Paris symbolizes the international support received.

The Canada Council granted funds for the photographic documentation survey carried out by Hilary Stewart. Ms. Stewart visited museums up and down the Fraser Valley, across the lower mainland of British Columbia, as well as every major museum on the continent possessing Northwest Coast material. The photographic archive assembled will be deposited at the University of British Columbia, Vancouver — providing a research resource for students for years to come.

Touring the exhibition to Vancouver, Toronto and Ottawa was made possible by the support of The National Museums Corporation, Ottawa. Ms. Claire Watson was particularly helpful. As far as I know no other exhibition organized in recent years in this country has been received with such enthusiasm. The Gallery is grateful for the enlightened programme of democratization and decentralization being developed through the efforts of The Honourable Hugh Faulkner, Secretary of State, who is responsible for The National Museums Corporation.

A study of the text which follows gives only a partial insight into the contribution of Wilson Duff, professor of anthropology of the University of British Columbia, who was the professional consultant to the exhibition. It was only after seeing a few of the pre-historic stone sculptures of British Columbia and studying his early researches (*Anthropology in British Columbia No. 5*, 1956) that I knew the exhibition could be assembled. Duff has given it form and coherence, tempering my enthusiasm with scholarly caution. His understanding is based upon more than twenty-five years of exposure to the art and culture of the Pacific Northwest; mine upon excitement of the unknown art I discovered for myself.

Hilary Stewart, unless otherwise noted, is responsible for the photographs, line drawings and other visual material. As the research assistant it was her responsibility to make the first evaluation of the singularity of the diverse forms she found.

There are so many other people to thank but they all know what they have contributed. Ms. Naomi Panchyson acted as executive secretary and was responsible for typing the catalogue and working out the logistics of travel. Mr. Jack Macgillivray, chief exhibition designer of The National Gallery of Canada, did a superb job of installation, and my thanks to Dr. Jean Sutherland Boggs for permitting us to use his services.

Richard Simmins

Victoria, British Columbia
March 4, 1975

preface

Hilary Stewart

Research is trudging through deep snow without boots in sub-zero weather with the wind in your face, or driving over a rough and desolate mountain road with the temperature reading 93 and your gas tank reading EMPTY. Research is locating a non-existent curator of a closed museum in a small town on a Sunday morning in a rainstorm, or working under photographic flood lamps in a climate-controlled storage area maintaining 50% humidity. Research is trying to photograph a bewitched ceremonial bowl that refuses to be photographed, or being locked in a museum storage attic after closing time.

For me, the very diversity, scope and uniqueness of IMAGES: STONE: B.C. seemed to be reflected in the task of researching and photographing the material for the exhibition.

From the mammoth domed and colonnaded Smithsonian Institute's Museum of Natural History in Washington, D.C., to the one roomed museum in a disused church in Lillooet, B.C., I searched for British Columbia stone sculpture that presented itself as a 'singular image', and I found it.

I found it in an amazing array of lithic art spread across the country and over the border. I found it in old varnished oak show cases, within plexiglass cubes on elegant pedestals, under dust enshrouded storage shelves of museum attics, in neatly labelled drawers inside locked steel containers, behind the doors of moth-proofed vaults, in vast display cases within marbled halls and on the mantlepieces of private homes.

With research came the excitement of discovery; a zoomorphic bowl, a figure or a finely carved club not previously published and hence almost totally unknown to the world at large.

Perhaps the greatest discovery was the 21" seated human figure bowl, the largest known. The B.C. Provincial Museum was given a replica of it in 1916, but the whereabouts of the original and information about it were unknown. I found it under a shelf in the storage annex of the Museum of the American Indian in the Bronx, New York.

A different kind of discovery was finding, through the lens of my camera, a new angle for a familiar piece, or touching with light the contours of a bold, carved face; the brow, the cheeks, the nose and the mouth; arched, curved, hollowed and shaped, dramatic and different with each angle of light. Light, like the sun, lifted these carved stone images from the dark of storage and gave them new life and new power to impress and mystify all over again. The camera snatched the impression and the mysticism in a fraction of a second and held on to it.

These sculptures in stone, often simple, sometimes powerful, always unique, ranged from a 1½" charm that lay small and gem-like in the palm of my hand to a massive carved mortar I was barely able to lift. Each singular piece of stone pulsed with vitality, vibrated energy. My hands, touching and turning a carving, became acutely aware of the sculptor and the hands that had originally created the piece. My mind became receptive, brittle, sensing the profound power the sculpture once commanded, often uneasily aware of the spirit still within the shaped stone.

Choosing these singular images and taking them from their attic anonymity, bringing them together for the first time and releasing them into a creative gallery setting is to give the eye, the mind and the soul a deep new experience of Indian splendour in stone.

introduction

IMAGES: A Way of Seeing
and A Way of Thinking

Images seem to speak to the eye, but they are really addressed to the mind. They are ways of thinking, in the guise of ways of seeing. The eye can sometimes be satisfied with form alone, but the mind can only be satisfied with meaning, which can be contemplated, more consciously or less, after the eye is closed.

Richard Simmins, in bringing these ancient stone images into the public eye in the Gallery, and Hilary Stewart, in seeking them out from distant attics and revealing them through the eye of her camera, have done their parts of our shared task. They have presented the images in a modern context and idiom as "art", which suggests a new way of seeing them. It remains for me to present them more fully to the mind. My part of the shared task, which might be called anthropology with a great deal of artistic licence, is to suggest ways of thinking about the images which will throw more light on their meanings.

The question I must ask is "what do the images mean?", and it is a question that demands answers in words, the language of thinking. It is a hazardous enterprise for one who values a reputation for scholarly discipline, because of course we do not really "know" what they "mean". It would be difficult enough — and terribly disconcerting — to explain what the images of our own culture "mean", because most of their meanings, most of the time, are left below or beyond the view of ordinary waking consciousness. It is doubly difficult to explain the images of a different culture, whose unspoken visions and premises we may not share. Not having the answers, and not even sure how to ask the questions, I am being presumptuous in saying anything at all about other peoples' symbols. But I think it is a risk worth taking, because it is being taken in an attempt to burst the chains of a long-felt frustration, a frustration which I am not alone in feeling. This stone art, Northwest Coast Indian art in general, and other arts equally remote from our own experience have remained as closed books for all too long, resisting our efforts to find the deeper meanings which we feel intuitively to be there. The best that I can offer are my most audacious imaginings about the meanings of the images. Imagination is what creates images in the first place; perhaps imagination and hard thinking are the keys to what they mean. The best test will be the degree to which my suggestions "open your eyes still further" to the stone art, and help you to "see it in a clearer light".

This exhibition had its moment of inception when the singular eye of Richard Simmins fell upon the powerful "Sechelt Image" in the Vancouver Centennial Museum, and saw it to be a singularly striking image and a great work of stone sculpture. A decade before that, a like response of the same aesthetic eye had initiated the "Arts of the Raven" exhibition at the Vancouver Art Gallery, the threshold over which Northwest Coast art had come into full recognition as "fine art" as well as "primitive art". Two decades before, I had looked in some detail at the prehistoric stone sculpture of southern British Columbia, although as archaeology rather than as art, and had written an encyclopedic study of it which was published by the Provincial Museum (Duff, 1956a). In the interim, my growing involvement with Northwest Coast art as high art and logic; not least, my participation with Bill Reid and Bill Holm in preparing the "Arts of the Raven" show, had sharpened my eye to its fuller meanings. When Simmins invited me to collaborate with him again on the present exhibition of stone sculpture, I found myself eager to give it a second look. The primary criterion of choice which he established at the beginning was one I found congenial: that each of the sculptures must strike the eye as a "singular image". The exhibition consists of 136 of the most singularly striking stone sculptures of the native Indian people of the pre-white Northwest Coast. It is not the total range, but it is a carefully chosen sample, and no effort was spared to bring them together.

I had also done a lot more thinking about the question of meaning in art. In my principal field of historic northern Northwest Coast art I had been engaged with my students in the discovery of a level of meaning of which we formerly had only hints. It is not something that invalidates previous understandings of its meanings: that it had stylized ways of representing animal forms, and that these served the purpose of family crests and referred back to myths. It is just that a great deal more seems to be going on than that. The additional level of meaning is a system of inner logic which resides in the style and in the internal structure of individual works of art. It is as though each is an equation wrapped as a single bundle. It constructs its statements upon the interplay between its parts, and between the literal and metaphoric meanings of its images. It uses inherent structural and conceptual dualisms in the artifacts and images: outside-inside, head-body, front-back, part-whole, and so on. Different artifact types, such as bowls, spoons, daggers, rattles, houseposts, lend their structure to the exploration of different kinds of equations. Some types, such as "coppers" and "soul catchers", are best understood as pure expressions of sets of relationship. It is a system of extreme complexity and powerful intellectual energy. That such a system exists is no longer surprising. The great French anthropologist Claude Lévi-Strauss has shown that the "savage mind" is really a scientific mind that uses natural images rather than abstract symbols to create what he calls a "science of the concrete". I would say that the artist-thinkers of the Northwest Coast had created a sort of "mathematics of the concrete", which by the time the white man arrived had become an "advanced mathematics". Northwest Coast art, in addition to its previously-recognized functions of representation and decoration, had come to be an arena for abstract thinking, a half-secret dialogue, a self-conscious system for diagramming logical paradoxes, and therefore a medium for exploring by analogy the living paradoxes in myth and life. Returning for a second look at the stone art, I found the same system of logic at work, especially in the less ancient forms from the northern coast such as tobacco mortars, but also in the more ancient sculptures from the southern parts of the province. My interpretations draw, at times, on examples which are not in stone, and on premises which have not yet been published elsewhere.

Let me go back to the beginning by admitting again bluntly that we do not have any way of "knowing" what the stone sculptures really "meant" to their makers and users. We have not observed them in use, or known anybody who has. Nor do the present generation of Indian people, their more rightful inheritors, have any better way of knowing their deeper meanings. The best we can do is make surmises, based upon what we know from archaeology, ethnography, and mythology, upon parallels with other objects of better known use and meaning, and upon our own perceptions of the images themselves. What we must acknowledge most of all is that our world of reality is very different from the world of reality within which they were created, and that the only certain area of overlap is that which results from a sharing of the concerns of the human condition. One such universal concern is sexuality; others are death, the perpetuation of life and self, and the basic shapes of order in human thought. But these, we must also notice, are matters about which man has often preserved his thoughts in stone.

The assumption is made that an image is "singular" because it touches some deep, unspoken perception of the truth of things. The seeing eye is not disconnected from the depths of the mind. There is no fixed dividing line between the seeing of the perceptive eye and the "seeing" of the conditioned mind; it is a matter of degree, of how conscious and explicit the meanings are made to become, of how hard one thinks about the subjects they touch. The assumption is made that the artist made his images touch upon these subjects on purpose.

How are the meanings to be found? It is easy enough to take the first step. We can usually put a word or a phrase to the image, even if it is only "face" or "seated human figure bowl". When the human figure is present we can usually recognize it as such, and may indulge in the spurious satisfaction of labelling it "anthropomorphic". But in most cases we do not know whether it was meant as being male or female (or perhaps both), a real character or a mythic one, a person or a category, or an equation using for its structure the parts and balances of the human body. When animal forms are present we can sometimes recognize a species, but in most cases have to retreat behind such question-begging words as "bird-like" and "quadruped". These of us who are expected to be experts may choose to use words like "zoomorphic", and interested laypersons may find a certain satisfaction in learning the experts' words, but it is a hollow satisfaction. Such words are masks to hide a lack of comprehension. They also hide their unexamined premise that the images simply "represent" things; that is, depict the creatures of nature and the imagination in more or less realistic ways. To ask "what does it represent?" and be satisfied with a single answer is not the same thing as asking "what does it mean?" The single answer may only be part of the story, a first level of meaning, or even the little truth that is a dangerous thing because it is a guise behind which the real meaning may be hiding. It could be said that the purpose of art is to provide guises for truths.

Could they not just be pleasing forms? Play with pure forms can produce singular images which require no further justification for existence, when that was really all that was going on. And stone's intractability is itself enough cause for some ambiguous images. Yet to fail to see beyond these determinants of the final image, I suspect, is to miss what is sometimes the most powerful core of the meaning. The missing part is the thinking part: the equation being made, the generalization. The meaning is in the relationships being expressed. The marriage of image and artifact creates a metaphor. A metaphor is a form of equation. An equation is a kind of proverb, whose meanings ripple out in resonating circles of relevant analogy to the limits of the mind. A stone image can be a chunk of truth.

But it is somehow putting it the wrong way to say that images contain meanings. Images contain apparent ambiguities. Images are seeming contradictions. Images hold ideas apart so that they can be seen held together. "Imaging" is reflecting. "Imaging" is relating. "Imaging" is recognizing. "Imaging" is "meaning". Images *are* meanings, which come out in the thinking.

STONE: The Medium and the Message

Stone is heavy. Stone is tough, unyielding, and everlasting. In the depths of man's mind, stone is associated with wholeness, self, truth, and eternity. When it is chosen as the medium for sculpture, stone's qualities and associations are incorporated as part of the meaning. Conversely, man's most enduring truths seem to demand preservation in stone.

Stone's hardness, toughness, and heaviness have always made it seem to man a proper medium for implements used for cutting, striking, crushing, and grinding. Hence the prominence in this exhibition of jade blades, hand hammers, sledge hammers, pile drivers, clubs, slave-killers, and mortars. The shape of each speaks of its use, which is what permits us to identify it. Each, that is to say, is an image of its own use. Each is an implement and, more important to us, an image of that implement, both at the same time. It may be the very image of all things that implement should ideally be, in which case we might call it "pure design" and a "type specimen". What we should not fail to notice is that the image seems at times to become more important than the implement itself, even to the point of rendering it disfunctional for its original use. A beautiful jade blade may be "larger than life": the very image of jade, and of chisel-form, and of the sawing and polishing techniques that brought it into creation; but it has become too good for everyday use as a chisel, it has become a "property celt", a "wealth object", a symbol. The most important use of some of man's implements is to carry his symbols.

Stone implements may bear additional images, or may become additional images, in which case we might call them "decorated" or "sculptured". A club may have a human head upon the handle; a sledge-hammer may be given eyes and a mouth, and become a "head". The most important thing to see is that a relationship exists between the image and the artifact. The image is "about" the artifact, it is a metaphorical restatement of a meaning of the artifact, it is another way of looking at the artifact. Artifact and image are metaphors of each other. Sharing the one-ness of the same piece of stone, they form an equation together. Again we must notice that the image sometimes becomes more important than the artifact which is its vehicle. The phalliform pestle is the very image of life's power and stone's hardness, but at the expense, I would imagine, of its everyday utility as a pestle. Many of the stone clubs have dropped all pretense of being functional as striking weapons, but bear images of much greater potential destructiveness. Again, the most important use of some of man's stone implements is to carry his images, and his equations. And in the equation, "stone" is usually one of the meanings.

Stone's toughness dictates the manner of its shaping, constraining the artist to make his statements as simply and directly as possible. It is a medium for blunt statements, threshold statements, even ambiguous statements. But conversely, when the artist has obviously taken great pains to coax a complex and perfect image out of the stubborn stone, one must understand that it is no casual statement he is making. The perfection of likeness of the twin stone masks, and of the four human faces on the large tobacco mortar, was no easy achievement, and is to be understood as the deliberate assertion of a similarity so exact as to be virtual sameness, outright identity. The two masks *are* one, the four faces *are* one, and that, I think, is the core of their meaning.

Stone's coarseness of texture, which urges simplicity of statement, can be turned into an asset by the artist who chooses to speak in puns and paradoxes by creating things that are two opposite things at the same time. Sculptural understatements can deliberately be left ambiguous. The Sechelt Image has just such an ultimate ambiguity: its mighty phallus is at the same time its partner, and they clasp each other in the same embrace. The human head on the club: is it a fetus or an old man? /No. 105/. And what of the little punned phallus-man, the part that is also a whole? /No. 66/.

Stone's lastingness makes it a proper medium for man's eternal truths. It is lasting in fact as well as in concept. The prehistoric stone sculptures found in the southern parts of the province are in truth the only surviving remnants of an ancient artistic tradition, the other expressions of which have perished. The meanings they convey did in fact prove undying; it only remains to decipher them. Stone means eternal. In the myths, the beings who are turned to stone live everlastingly as reminders of the circumstances that caused their transformation, and of their lasting implications for man. The association of stone with eternity is surely universal: think of gravestones, the philosophers' stone, the Stone of Scone, the Rock of Ages. Artists who find universal truths choose to preserve them in stone. We may see this in masterpieces for which stone was clearly a "chosen" medium, such as the matched pair of stone masks. One such truth, perhaps, is the paradox that oppositeness amounts to the same thing as sameness.

To select stone, the medium of eternity, is to deny time and reject death. Our own culture has used gravestones and stone statues to preserve forever the memories and images of men. But to the artists who created the images in this exhibit, the surest denial of death seems to have been in the celebration of the origins of life: the dominant images are of sex, and forms of life, and eyes. The ancient seated human figure bowls, especially, seem to have been associated with woman's puberty, the onset of her awesome power to bring forth renewed human life. Stone is about life and death. Stone is about time. If a club could be devised to kill death, it would be made of stone. If a design could be devised to thwart time, it would exist in stone.

BC: Place and Time: One Land, Two Worlds

"British Columbia" is an image of place which we have imprinted on this land, and "Before Christ" an image of time. As a world of reality, British Columbia is scarcely one century old. The earlier Indian world of reality stretched back at least a hundred centuries. It was indeed a world before Christ, a world of different images, a world of different time. The names of its philosophers are long forgotten, but the shapes of a few of their thoughts have survived in stone.

IMAGES: STONE: BC can be viewed as a retrospective show of the best surviving works of the artists of the last thirty centuries of that other world of time. We have chosen 136 of what seem to us to be their most singular images, and brought them together into one assemblage. The map shows the places where they have been found. Such information as we have on their ages is given in the catalogue. It is not much, but is improving with the growth of disciplined archaeology. Perhaps it is sufficient for the present purpose of seeing the broad patterns. In general, the images of the southern regions dominated by the Fraser River seem "of an older period" than those of the northern regions dominated by the Skeena River. It is as though we are able to discern two great surges of thought in art: one culminating about twenty centuries ago in the emergence of the seated human figure bowls, and the other, some time later in the north, culminating in the tobacco mortars and stone masks. The second surge wears the style of historic northern Northwest Coast art, that great creative explosion which helped to fill the world's museums, and reminds us that the stone images alone are meagre indeed as records of that abundant life. In between the two periods, at least in time, are the magic, Hagwilget clubs from the upper Skeena River. If the bowls and mortars are the Indian artists' parables on woman and her gift of life, these are their most revealing parables on man and his burden of power.

Threads of imagery and of logic seem to run through the entire assemblage, and seem even to show the different kinds of images to be contributions to a single, continuing dialogue. Its underlying imagery, like the Yin and Yang of China, seems to be that of the fundamental duality of sex. Its metaphors are borrowed from animal forms and from the human body; phallic images paired with vulvic images. The ambiguous rattlesnake and owl of the south are succeeded by the doubly-ambiguous "Frog" and "Hawk" of the north, but the logic seems to be the same, just pushed another step forward. It is almost as though our retrospective exhibition were showing the periods of a single artist through his long career.

That artist took a pride in his artifacts, making them exquisite mediators between the hand and the task at hand, and pleasing to the eye and mind as well. Not only did he make his artifacts into their own best images; he also made them the vehicles for his more powerful and general mental images, using them as parables for his general principles and higher purposes, and as blackboards for his logical equations. The ancestral pair of artifact types seems to have been the mortar and pestle, together grinding nature's seeds into the food of human life. Pestles were paradoxes, because they could also be used as hammers, and even as clubs for killing. His hammers and clubs became the images of his male power, but the paradox remained forever with him in his ambivalence whether to use his power to give life or bring death. The image of the mortar as the "vessel of life" remained with him in his mind, but characteristically, he also conceived the idea that it was somehow the opposite. He exorcised the spectre of the rattlesnake-vessel by cancelling death out completely on the northern Frog-vessel, but secretly he knew that both were really figments of his own imagination. On some of his artifact types, the images took over completely. Some of the seated human figure bowls (like No. 52) are bowls in name only, which may mean that they have become "vessel" in general. Some of his hammers (like No. 83) are hammers in name only, the secret meaning of which may be that they are pure pestles once again. Some of the clubs (like No. 105) became pure threats. Some of the mortars became promises of pure satiation (like No. 124), or pure tranquillity (No. 134).

For the additional images to superimpose on his artifacts, he looked to the natural world and to his own body. He seems to have drawn from nature an analogy he could apply to himself, the species concept. He took animal species as guardian spirits or as family crests, as if to assure himself that he shared the eagles' certainty that their eggs would hatch eagles, and the bears' certainty that their offspring would indeed be

20

bear cubs. Deep down, the problem seems to have worried him, because he also borrowed from nature images of ambiguity like the owl, which sees in darkness, and the snake, which can swallow things bigger than itself, and the frog, which seems to know no sex but multiplies with every rain. He tried to think his way through the ambiguities by halfing them and doubling them, creating monsters of his own devising which should be able to have it both ways, like "Hawk" and "Frog". His animal metaphors became equations as well as names.

The self-images he took from his own body were not total portraits but parts and their attributes. Throughout most of his career his major body-images were sexual, and mostly metaphoric. In his equations inverting the role of "part" and "whole", he usually chose the sexual part. We have long suspected him of some amount of phallic symbolism, because he sometimes made explicit male erections (like Nos. 74 and 75). The explicit ones I call "phalliform", the metaphoric ones, just "phallic". What we do not seem to have recognized until now is that the opposite is equally true. While it presents a more difficult problem of depiction, a small number of the images can be said to be "vulviform" (like Nos. 28 and 29), and many more just "vulvic". The pairing of the two seems to be his basic image of the human condition, the "big bang" of life itself, like the Yin and Yang of China, the lingam-yoni of India, and perhaps even the Gothic arch and steeple of Europe.

What he was seeking most of all was order, balance, mediation, wisdom. His own two hands provided one image of balance, but not so purely as his own two eyes, because he knew that the most basic problem of all is that of self-recognition. Images of eyes are found throughout his career, from the spindle whorl /No. 3/ to the twin stone masks. In my view, the triumphs of his early period were the tranquil little lullaby of pure form /No. 6/, and the ferocious seated human figure bowl with rattlesnakes /No. 30/. The intensity of his middle period burns most brightly in two of the stone clubs /Nos. 101 and 105/. In the wisdom of age, he rested his case in the tranquil four-faced tobacco mortar /No. 134/, and showed his own mature self-image in the twin stone masks. Throughout his career he showed a recognition of the real adversary: Time. On that seated human figure bowl, it is only the rattlesnake's eyes that are open. Those clubs seem to be in a constant state of oscillating double-reversal, faster than the snake's strike, or the frog's tongue. The eyes on the masks are winking at each other. They see that Time is not so much a problem as a necessary part of the pattern. They see the adversary not as an enemy, but as a partner, and a twin.

We do not know the name of the maker of the masks, nor any of that artist's earlier names. But I think I know his last one: Edenshaw.

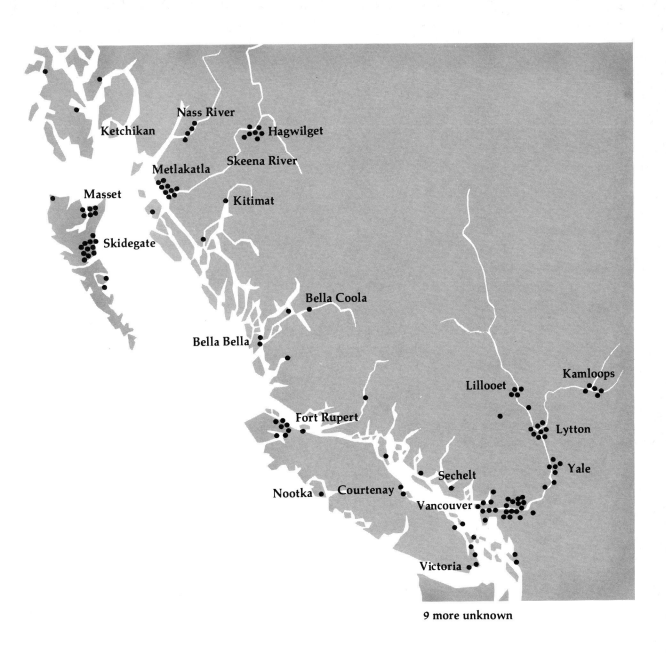

Nass River
Ketchikan
Hagwilget
Skeena River
Metlakatla
Kitimat
Masset
Skidegate
Bella Coola
Bella Bella
Kamloops
Lillooet
Lytton
Fort Rupert
Yale
Sechelt
Nootka
Courtenay
Vancouver
Victoria

9 more unknown

Locations where Images were found

The Criterion and the Sample

Another way of viewing this exhibition is as part of the dialogue between art and archaeology. Archaeologists cannot usually confine their view to the "singular images" of the cultures they study, and art historians are not yet in the habit of seeing real art in archaeological assemblages. This is a new blend. It is perhaps more art than archaeology, since it is more an exhibit of images than of artifacts as such, and since the primary criterion is an aesthetic one. It does not include all of the images we found, but only those which we see as "singular images". The criterion is admittedly a subjective one, and the sample would meet nobody's test of exhaustiveness but our own. But having established the criterion, we spared no efforts to assemble the best possible sample. Lenders have been incredibly generous. We know of very few other images which would have met the criterion but were unavailable for loan. In that sense, it is a fair sample.

Still another way of viewing these 136 pieces of sculpture, however, is as a false and artificial concentration of sacred images which were originally far separate in space and time. Such medicine was never meant to be taken in such strong doses. This is a highly concentrated residue, like a snowman made from the black crust on the springtime remnants of Ottawa's winter snow. Most of these images were meant to be glimpsed only occasionally, in ritual circumstances, in the hands of trusted practitioners. If they seem to deal obsessively with heavy subjects such as sex and death, it is partly because of what we have done to them: gathered the stone residue of thirty centuries from a wide area, and assembled it under lights. The accumulated power that these have held should surely blow the mind. It is perhaps a mercy that we glimpse their meanings only faintly. But it is a private and secret place that we have stumbled into. In that sense, it is not a fair sample.

And yet another way of looking at IMAGES: STONE: BC is as part of the long overdue granting of recognition to the full and complete humanity of the people who originally lived here. "Before Christ" was an image of judgement as well as of time, which somehow made it easier to dispossess them of their world. They were "heathens", "primitives", not yet knowing God's command to subjugate the earth. Those verdicts are

52
Seated Human Figure Bowl

58
Sawn Nephrite

59
Nephrite Blade

90
**Hafted Hammer:
The "Hawk" that eats Whales**

97
**Pile Driver:
Dogfish Head**

101
Stone Club

105
Stone Club

124
Tobacco Mortar: Frog

127
**Tobacco Mortar:
Frog, Seal and Human**

135
Mask

136
Mask

images of our own making and for our own contemplation, and they are changing in the contemplation. With the "Arts of the Raven" show, we granted their artists credence as producers of high art. Perhaps our eyes were not even then completely open. With this exhibition we come a step further, and begin to grant their artist-philosophers credence as people of intellect and mature wisdom. To the existing proof of the prior claim and Indian presence in Canada may be added, however poorly understood, this evidence of thirty centuries of hard thinking.

Postscript

Images are for contemplation. One of the ingredients of contemplation is time. Time and contemplation were also ingredients in the preparation of IMAGES: STONE: BC, and have yielded insights and meanings far beyond those which were foreseen at the beginning. To close my introduction, let me suggest some ways of seeing deeper into a few of the stone images.

One kind of contemplation comes out of seeing and thinking at the same time. Let me suggest a way of "seeing" the masterpiece of ancient stone clubs from Hagwilget, the one I call Death-Bringer /No. 105/. Think of the stone clubs as thinking about themselves. Think of them as images for the contemplation of all things associated with clubs, and man's uses of clubs, and stone. A club is a supremely ambiguous thing: a tool for life-taking as well as life-preserving. Its controlling image, from among man's stock of self-images, would seem on existing evidence to be the phallus. A phallus is also a supremely ambiguous thing: equal parts life-maker and death-maker; equal parts "pestle" and "dagger"; the one, in woman's hand, a life-maker; the other, in man's hand, a life-waster. The stone-club has two ends: think of the handle and blade as the two sides of an equation. On the handle is a very strange human head. Is it a new infant, eyes not yet open to life? Or is it an old, old man, eyes closing for death? Is this the moment of "first gasp", or of "last gasp"? Or is it somehow meant as both, and therefore all the time and all the gasps between them? On the blade is something equally ambiguous. Is it "sword" or "pestle"? Is it the sting that means death, or the touch that means life? Is it cold, hard murder, or "killing me softly"? The element that activates the whole equation is a living hand on the handle. That particular handle, clenched in a male hand, would be an expression of the opposite of love: those eyes would be choked closed rather than coaxed open. The image is in stone, a message for all time, and open eyes.

There is another kind of contemplation that comes out of closing the eyes, then feeling and thinking at the same time. Our hands, in some sense, have eyes and minds of their own. I have had the privilege of being able to handle the stone images: to heft Death-Bringer in my right hand, to cradle No. 29, the little life-form bowl, in my left. I can testify that they both "feel good" in equal ways. There is also something of the feel of life in hefting the Shark pile-driver /No. 97/, and the Sechelt Image. The T-shaped hand maul /No. 78/ feels doubly good to the grip, for all the world like "holding hands".

Let me suggest an example of the kind of contemplation that rests primarily in the hand: /No. 6/, the smooth little soap-stone "whatsit", twenty centuries old and two inches long, which is shown upright and face-on in Plate 6 a. Think of it as an image to be caressed in the hand, and read as in Braille. Run sensitive mental fingertips along its top, and front, and ends, and back, and bottom, and front again. It will not let you down. Top and front feel like one smooth, concave trip, swooping gently upwards, gathering equally into two separate tips which are not quite points. Both ends — not really ends — rise equally up and out and back. On the back, the finger finds an accented central half, a step, which is in turn a threshold to a portal on the bottom, an invitation around to the front again, and up, and out both ways again. The whole is no more than a smooth pebble, a light and easy handful, knowing no higher purpose than to give pleasure to the touch. The image is in stone, a gentle everlasting thrill, a pet, a lullaby.

Two kinds of contemplation: the one, "eyes open", the other, "eyes closed". One sees how it is to be human. The other feels how it is to be human. They are twin stone faces, recognizing each other in each other.

images
stone
b.c.

Image of Strength

Kwakiutl man lifting a strength-testing stone. From a photograph by W. Duff at Smith Inlet in 1956.

1

The Sechelt Image

Heavy oval boulders were hoisted as feats of male strength by some of the Salish and Kwakiutl people, sometimes at betrothal ceremonies. This one seems to be the very image of masculine strength, stated in the metaphor of sex. His head is powerfully masculine, and he clasps a huge phallus; the whole boulder, seen backwards and upside down, is phallic in form. But the image is still more complex than that: it shows also its opposite. Below the phallus is a vulva. The phallus has arms, which clasp the man. His ambiguity is absolute: "male strength" is also "mother and child".

2
The Most Ancient Image

Tiny, worn, animal-form, thirty centuries old, from a site on the Fraser Canyon that enjoyed almost a hundred centuries of Indian occupation.

3

Spindle Whorl: Snakes and Eyes

Spindle whorls, usually made of wood, were used by the Salish people in transforming mountain goat wool into robes. This one, perhaps a dozen centuries old, is the image of spinning. On the front, the clearest eye is the one in the centre, through which the spindle passes (it was also going to be the mouth of an oval face); the rest twirl dizzily. On the back, in a sea of eyes, two entwining serpents face each other, as on Mercury's staff, with a third between.

4
Double Labret

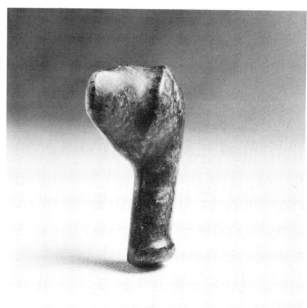

5
Labret with Appendage

6
Pure Form ("Whatsit")

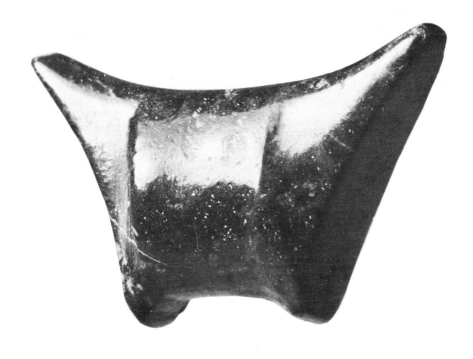

Ancient Abstractions

These tiny abstract sculptures are about twenty centuries old.
We know that the labret was an ornament worn on the mid-
line of the body, through a perforation in the lower lip; most
likely, as in more recent times on the northern coast, by women.
We do not know how "whatsits" were used. These ones, the
masterpieces and very images of their kinds, may be expressions in pure form of their most essential meanings. Each of
them speaks of perfect bilateral balance. The labrets convey
hints of the sexual duality. The pure form "whatsit" resists all
specific suggestions as to use and image, but if viewed as an
idealized generalization is the very model of balance and up-
rightness.

Images of Man

Man's images, in one sense or another, are self-images. The sculptor, we assume, was male. But what are "images"? Images are visual metaphors. Man's images are metaphoric statements of something about himself. So it was through thirty centuries until the next insistent question recognized itself in the twin stone masks: What is metaphor? Is it an image of something the same, or something opposite? Male, or female? Part, or whole? Or neither? Or both? Or that-which-is-common-to-all, like human-form, face, eye?

7

Hunchback Man

8

Human Figure

9

Head

10
Head

11
Head

12

Face

13

Crouching Man

14

Head with Beard

Fonts of Life:
Bowls in Life Forms

15
Animal-form Bowl

16
Paint Mortar: "Diving Porpoise"

A study of the prehistoric stone sculpture of the Fraser River and Gulf of Georgia twenty years ago showed the dominant forms to be vessels in a wide variety of life forms, culminating in the predominant "seated human figure bowls". While some of the simpler, ancestral types may have been paint mortars or, possibly, oil lamps, most of the bowls of animal and human form are assumed to have been used for ritual purposes,

17

Animal-form Bowl

holding sacred oil, powder, or water. The seated human figure bowls, at least, have been associated with girls' puberty rites, which were of exceedingly great importance in western North America.

Some of the animal-form bowls can be identified as specific animals such as owl, seal, and turtle, but many cannot. Some have heads at both ends. A small number are explicitly vulviform. It is suggested that the controlling image is that of female sexuality, and that the owls, seals, and turtles had some punned or metaphoric association with that image. A more usual explanation is that they may have represented "guardian spirits" of the owner, but that may be saying the same thing in a different way.

18

Animal-form Bowl

A few of the bowls are in the tops or backs of human heads, and a few are in the bellies of reclining human figures. These may be seen as conceptual steps in the development of the ultimate type, the seated human figure bowl.

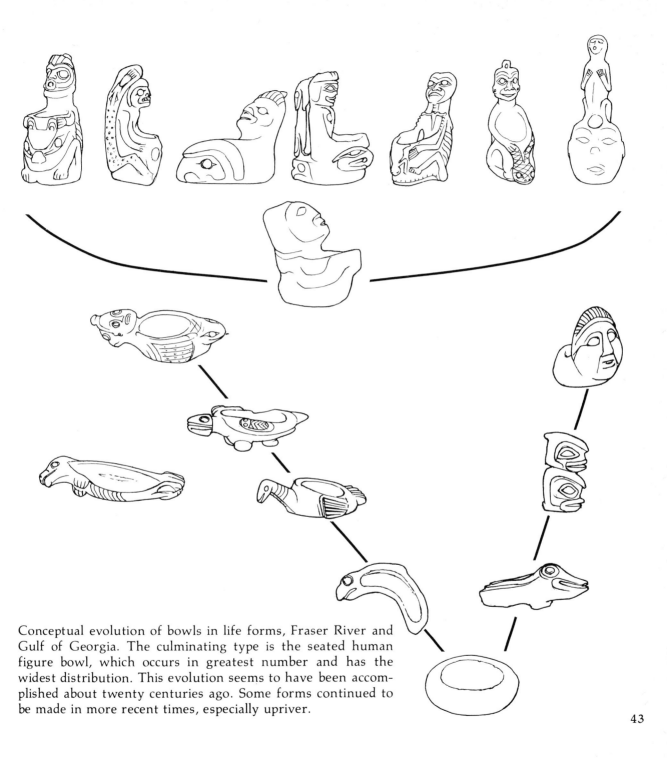

Conceptual evolution of bowls in life forms, Fraser River and Gulf of Georgia. The culminating type is the seated human figure bowl, which occurs in greatest number and has the widest distribution. This evolution seems to have been accomplished about twenty centuries ago. Some forms continued to be made in more recent times, especially upriver.

19
Bowl: Owl

20
Bowl: Bird

21

Bowl: Turtle with Beetles

22

Bowl: Square Turtle

23
Bowl: Twin Heads

24
Bowl in Head

25
Bowl in Head

26
Bowl Behind Face

27
Bowl with Two Faces

Vulviform Vessels

28
Bowl: Vulviform Seal

This charming little bowl or palette, five inches long, was found near Yale on the Fraser River, and seems to represent a seal. Its vulvic shape is echoed in many grease dishes made of wood from the northern Northwest Coast, which also represent seals. It is a tempting suggestion that "seal" is an ancient metaphor for vulva.

29

Bowl: Vulviform, with Two Faces

This smooth little vessel fits snugly into the left hand. It was excavated from a housepit near Lillooet, and is about fifteen centuries old. Upright, it is an open, lipped bowl. Upside down, it is a closed, mounded cleft. The faces on the ends may represent owls, or may be generically human. The two faces, in some sense, are the same (and so are the two faces on the ends of seated human figure bowls such as /No. 30/. Like the seal dish, it is in a sense a part without the whole.

Image: Stone: BC. One land, two worlds. One pebble of soapstone, two imprints of man. Fifteen centuries after the Indian artist had fashioned the pebble into his image, the archaeologist named it with his code, fashioned out of the alphabet, map squares, and a system of numeration.

Fonts of Life:
Seated Human Figure Bowls

. . . at the end of the puberty ceremonies the shaman led the girl back from seclusion in grand procession. He carried a dish called tsuqta'n, which is carved out of steatite, in one hand. The dish represents a woman giving birth to a child, along whose back a snake crawls. The child's back is hollowed out and serves as a receptacle for water. In the other hand the shaman carries certain herbs. When they returned to the village the herbs were put into the dish, and the girl was sprinkled with the water contained in the dish, the shaman praying at the same time for her to have many children.

Professor Boas published this account, referring to the Indian people of the Yale area, in 1890 (p. 90, fn.). He obtained the information from Mr. J. W. Mackay, an Indian agent. Professor Hill-Tout received similar information on the seated human figure bowl /No. 57/ found in an Indian burial ground at Kamloops: it was said by the Indians to have been used in girls' puberty ceremonies, the shaman sprinkling her with its sacred water on her return from seclusion in the woods. This most remarkable form of prehistoric sculpture seems therefore to have still been in use among the Interior Salish people in recent times.

Distribution

The number of known seated human figure bowls is about sixty; they are the most numerous and widespread of the southern forms of stone sculpture. Their distribution centres on the mouth of the Fraser River, extending to Vancouver Island from Victoria to Courtenay, and upriver as far as Lillooet and Kamloops. As the chart shows, they represent the culmination of an evolution of bowl forms, which become increasingly complex in image and also, presumably, in meaning. They are made predominantly of steatite (soapstone), which occurs as natural boulders in the Fraser River above Hope. West of that point about half are made of poorer rock, but the best ones are of soapstone, and some bear images of rattlesnakes, which do not occur on the coast. The artists who made the best ones seem therefore to have been upriver people, and the style seems to have reached its high point in a number of small and complex bowls from the vicinity of Lytton.

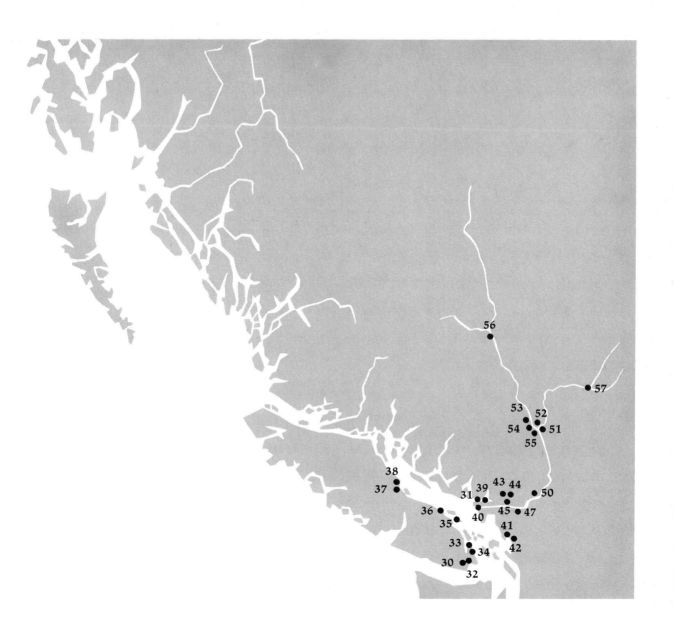

Locations where Seated Human Figure Bowls were found

Despite a remarkable diversity of detail, these images show a uniformity of concept throughout their range, which suggests a uniformity of use and meaning. A sitting or kneeling human figure, large head tilted slightly back, holds a bowl in its arms and between its legs. The bowl, as a bowl, is often very small or otherwise inefficient, as though the concept is more important than the fact. Many are embellished with animal forms: rattlesnakes, toads, owl-like birds; on the head, back, and breast of the human, but mostly on the front of the bowl, where the animal face is sometimes monstrous and unidentifiable. Backbones, shoulder-blades, and ribs are often shown, as though the human were starved, although the faces, often singing, seem full and healthy. Most have some form of headdress or hair ornament.

Age

At least three /31, 39, 40/ of the seated human figure bowls have been found in or upon the famous Marpole site, on the north arm of the Fraser River in the city of Vancouver, which indicates that they were in existence between 2500 and 1500 years ago, when the site was a thriving village. One of these, the "Marpole Image", is here assumed to be a sort of prototype. It was found in 1930 in the midden and associated with a burial. The others have been found in a wide range of unexpected locations. Upriver, they have been found in association with burials, some of which show evidence of much antiquity. In the lower Fraser Valley and on Vancouver Island, they have sometimes been found in remote spots, occasionally in pairs and occasionally broken and discoloured by heat, as though burned on the owner's death. Very few came from habitation sites which would reveal their archaeological context and age. A few have been purchased from Indian people, but in none of these cases were they family heirlooms of known use and meaning. The impression is that they were little used in historic times, and their meaning was a secret known only to a few.

Use

On the basis of all available ethnographic information, the earlier study (Duff, 1956a) concluded that seated human figure bowls had not been used as lamps, mortars, or food vessels, but as ritual and divining vessels by shamans and ritualists. The Salish people of the area had highly developed powers of clairvoyance and prophecy. Their ritualists performed (and still perform) rites of purification and cleansing for individuals at different stages of their lives. One of the most important of such times was the onset of female puberty, when the woman became able to bring forth new life. Everywhere in western North America this power was mightily venerated. The girl was secluded for weeks or months, underwent tests and training, and was reintroduced into society in the new role and with new respect. It seems wholly appropriate to conclude that the most remarkable stone sculptures of the area are associated with this veneration of life, and are in that sense sacred art.

Meaning

IMAGES: STONE: B.C. is, among other things, a study of the manner in which art conveys meaning; it is an enquiry into the process of "imaging". The assumption is that the image is a metaphorical restatement of an essential meaning of the artifact. The "seated human figure bowl" seems to be the product of a complex evolution of form, and therefore a complex evolution of idea. Given what is known of their use, one might expect that the ideas have something to do with life-bringing and its consequences. One might expect them to show the most powerful images of that culture, since they deal with its most powerful dilemma. One might expect those images to appear also in other parts of the culture, as for example in its myths.

What, in that context, do the seated human figure bowls "mean"? The question can be answered at two levels — such is the nature of art — one rather easy, the other much more difficult and potentially disquieting.

The easier question to ask is "what do the images represent?" One of the answers, surprisingly but undeniably, is "rattlesnakes". In nature, rattlesnakes do not occur west of Lytton. Least of all do they occur in rose gardens in Victoria, where /No. 30/ was unearthed in 1960. This is one of the largest and most terribly powerful of all the seated human figure bowls. Down its back, upside down, is as emphatic a depiction of a rattlesnake as one could possibly wish. The monstrous, wide-eyed face on the front of the bowl is also identified as rattlesnake by two tails with rattles extending back along the flanks of the human figure. If the image is "about" the bowl, that bowl, metaphorically, is a "rattlesnake mouth". The cheeks of the human figure are two bulgy ridges converging on the

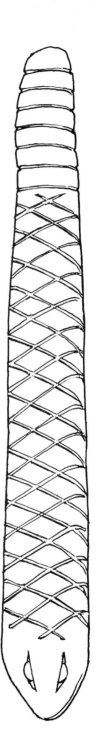

30
**Seated Human Figure Bowl
with Rattlesnakes (Victoria)**

mouth. By analogy with other seated human figure bowls, these can also be read as rattlesnakes, which makes that mouth, in a similar sense, a "rattlesnake mouth". Similar depictions of rattlesnakes are found on some of the other bowls, including /No. 53/ from Rattlesnake Flat at Lytton, where the creatures more naturally occur, and where quite conceivably the Victoria bowl was carved. One wonders what mental image the people of Victoria conjured up about that serpent, and what its symbolic meaning came to be.

It is also easy to recognize that the main figure on these bowls represents a human being. None of them show male sexual characteristics. All of them, if only in the metaphor of the vessel in the belly, could be considered female; unless, as in the instance of the Sechelt Image, they are somehow meant to have the sexual attributes of both.

We can also recognize some of the other animals which adorn the bowls. A few are monstrous, beak-nosed creatures that resist identification, but we can find some which are clearly frogs or toads and some which are birds, most likely owls. The Salish people's regard for snakes, and frogs, and owls was rather like our own, except that it struck home with much more force. Snakes and frogs were somehow poisonous. Owls were death-omens, ghosts, disembodied spirits. These are strange images to find adorning fonts of life, unless we invoke a logic of opposites. It is perhaps easier to postulate that these creatures may have represented the "guardian spirits" of the owners of the bowls. And that would be as far as our usual kind of interpretation would take us into the "meaning" of the images.

To persist in digging deeper into the meanings of this art is in a sense a sacrilege, and a violation of its purpose, because what we are attempting to do is elucidate that which should only be hinted at, lay bare the very things which art exists to disguise. Art seems to deal with that which is terrifying and that which is taboo, and it does it in the guise of dealing with that which is familiar and controllable. We penetrate its guises at our own peril, and most of the time, the best common sense is not to try. But the terrifying and the taboo — in a word, the sacred — will not be ignored, and it seems to be the mission of great artists to show us how to come to terms with them.

One of the keys to the deeper understanding of a people's

art may lie in the images in their myths. Myth, like art, seems to have as its hidden agenda the problem of coming to terms with the terrible dilemmas of the human condition. As Professor Levi-Strauss has taught us, the provisional answers lie in the logic implicit in the resolution of the myths.

James Teit published a myth of the Thompson Indians, who are the people of the Lytton area, which seems to be dealing with the logic and dilemmas of sexual relationships.[1] It is about an old woman, Xolakwaxa, who in effect tests out every logical antithesis of woman-ness, finds them thwarted by a committee of culture heroes, and, the point established, turns to stone. The old lady in the myth developed a cannibalistic hunger to eat the hearts of her own people. She sharpened her legs to awl-like points with four whetstones, killed babies by piercing their bellies, and ate their hearts. Four culture heroes, Coyote, Fox, Wolf, and Lynx, followed her next-to-invisible tracks, and when they caught up with her, she threw herself down on her back, sharpened legs in the air, and offered them her vulva:

When they drew near, she said to them, "I want a man. Come here and have connection with me." She intended to kill them. They answered, "We will satisfy you. Have patience." Fox said, "I do not like those awl-like pointed legs of hers: she may pierce us with them." Wolf said, "I am not afraid: I will go first." Coyote said, "That is Xolakwaxa; she intends to kill us. The danger is not with her legs, but with her privates, which bite and are poisonous, like the head of a rattlesnake. With them she intends to kill us. I will go first as I am the most knowing one." He sharpened a short stick at both ends, went up to the woman, and, when she tried to bite off his privates with hers, he placed the stick so that they could not shut. Now the others also had connection with her, and, when they were through, Coyote transformed her into stone, saying, "You will henceforth be a stone, and you and this place will be called Nkaxwil. You will remain with your privates open."

[1] J. A. Teit, "The Mythology of the Thompson Indians," 1912, p. 366; quoted and analyzed by M. Calkowski, "Cannibalism and Infertility among the Lillooet, Thompson, and Shuswap: The Shaman as Sexual Mediator," M. A. Thesis, 1974.

The seated human figure bowls may well be seen as portraits of Nkaxwil, reminders of the truth that the vulva is forever a thing of life, not death, whatever the intention. Maybe that is the point that the shamans who owned them were trying to impress upon young women at puberty. But just in case man's secret fear is true, that the vulva, like the toothed and poisonous rattlesnake head, contains a built-in double-negative lie, at least we know the logical shape of the answer: a bi-pointed stick. That shape gives men the power to subdue the fiercest mouths. The story is told of the Thompson Indian grizzly bear hunter who had one made of bone, which he thrust crosswise into the bear's gaping mouth, then killed the distracted beast with a stone club (Teit, *The Thompson Indians*, p. 249; quoted and analyzed in Calkowski, 1974, p. 86). There is a deep and complex logic in the structure of that image, a conformation of logic which Northwest Coast artists seem to have used as the ground-plan for many of their greatest works. It is a form of equation which can be clothed in innumerable images. Its essential structure is that of a figure-eight with a double-twist built in, that of a pair of linked Mobius strips. I suspect that it is the essential shape of Levi-Strauss' myth formula, and that it is the logical underpinning of the ancient arrangement known as the Quaternity.

A bi-pointed, negative stick set crosswise in a double-dangerous, positive mouth. Make the points of the stick the sharpest conceivable points. Make the teeth the sharpest conceivable teeth, and the mouth the largest conceivable mouth, so large that it can swallow itself. Make the positive and negative the two ends of every continuum, the two sides of every conceivable binary opposition. You have the makings of the universal equation. You have another version of Yin plus Yang equals Tao. I suspect that you have another version of the innocuous little equal-sign in e "equals" mc^2.

A bi-pointed male stick set crosswise into a doubly-ambiguous female mouth, made eternal in stone. That is the image provided by the myth. That is the parable of the way things are for man. That is one cloak of the frame of logic by which humanity "sees" its world. I suspect that the logic of the Salish grizzly bear hunter is no more than a mirror image of that of the Nootka whaler, and of the Spanish bull fighter. The image is no more than a proverb: its essence of meaning is not in its content but in its structure: its magic is that it rings true for all things of like conformation.

One aspect of the question has to do with sex. Some of the images are phalliform or vulviform, and most are just a metaphoric step removed: phallic or vulvic. Sex is perhaps the second most important binary opposition in the human condition. But something even more fundamental seems to be going on: the making of sense out of things. It has to do with logic. Things are only seen in the mirror of their opposites. We are constantly being reminded that the opposite is equally true. Tacked on to the bi-phallic club, life-at-both-ends, is an owl-like image of death. Superimposed upon the Sechelt Image of male "strength" is an image of "mother and child". The final seated human figure bowl on our list, /No. 57/ from Kamloops, is said to represent a woman giving birth, but its total outline is phalliform. The masterpiece of slope-handled hammers /No. 82/, has a magnificent handle which is phallic above, vulvic below. Sex is surely important, but the art seems to be striving to express something even more important: balance. When it guises itself in images, including sexual images, the important thing is that they must acknowledge their opposites, and balance. In pure form, as in the little "whatsit" /No. 6/, the image is of balance pure and simple.

But the rattlesnake in the Garden of Victoria brings back the realization that it has to do with one thing more. It is not just a question of male and female, the ambivalent vulva and man's logical response, but of life and death. Man seems to see the vulva, font of life, as wearing two faces. If we are to believe the little life-form bowl /No. 29/, they are very much the same, but can be seen only one at a time. When you are seeing one, you cannot see the other. The final limitation is in the eye, behind the eye. When it is "seeing" one thing, it is blind to its opposite. The final question is about the divine spark that joins seeing and "seeing". The very image of "seeing" is not the vulva but the eye. Life is a pair of twin stone masks which are the very same but have opposite eyes. They are blind to each other's points of view, but both of them recognize that they are wearing an equal share of Frog's half-ambivalent, half-enigmatic smile.

31

Seated Human Figure Bowl: The Marpole Image

August 25, 1930. Found the idol . . . approximately 4 feet down and 1 foot up /from the bottom of the midden/ about 8 feet west of the big maple. It lay on its side on a low rough cairn of boulders and earth, perhaps 4 feet across at the base. The striped shell-layers of the later accumulations rose a little overhead. On a slab on the cairn's top beside the idol lay the shoulder blade of some animal. Inside the cairn, in a conical mass of mixed yellow drift and black midden soil, was an "unwrapped" skeleton — bones very clean and white. One arm seemed small and undeveloped. At its wrist was a bone chisel. No trace of paint on idol. Pretty crude conventionalization, but looks rather like a little bear with a man's face holding out a saucer. A stumpy little tail in the usual place.

This extract from the field notes of Mr. Herman Leisk (courtesy Vancouver Centennial Museum, transcribed from the originals by Gordon Stanley) establishes that the Marpole Image was found in the midden of DhRs 1, the well-known Marpole (Eburne) site on the north arm of the Fraser at the south end of Granville Street in Vancouver. Its age seems therefore likely to be more than 2000 years, and it may be considered as a simple prototype of the seated human figure bowls.

32
**Seated Human Figure Bowl
(Victoria)**

33
**Seated Human Figure Bowl
(Sidney)**

34

Seated Human Figure Bowl (North Saanich)

35
**Seated Human Figure Bowl
(Kuper Island)**

36
**Seated Human Figure Bowl
(Nanaimo)**

37
Seated Human Figure Bowl (Royston)

38
Seated Human Figure Bowl (Courtenay)

65

39

Seated Human Figure Bowl
(Marpole)

40

Seated Human Figure Bowl
(Marpole)

41

Seated Human Figure Bowl

42

Seated Human Figure Bowl (Lummi)

43

Seated Human Figure Bowl (Haney)

This is a good bowl for seeing, and also, perhaps, a good one for thinking. Down the back are two snakes, eating. Or is it meant to be one snake, eating itself from the tail? On the breast is another snake. Or is it meant to be the same snake, eating the human? On the top, the human looks forward; on the bottom, the owl looks backward. And on the front of the bowl is a monster: a bit like the human, a bit like the owl, a bit like the snake. Is it eating its own beak? Is it eating itself? All things considered, is this a self-eating bowl?

69

44
Seated Human Figure Bowl
(Webster's Corners)

45
Seated Human Figure Bowl
(Webster's Corners)

46
Head of Seated Human Figure Bowl (Chilliwack)

47
Body of Seated Human Figure Bowl (Chilliwack)

In the process of bringing this exhibition together, this head and this body were re-united; the one from a "private collection", and the other from "dead storage" in the Laboratory of Archaeology. Was the figure broken and burned on the owner's death? Do they really belong together?

48
**Head of Seated
Human Figure Bowl**

49
Seated Human Figure Bowl

50
Seated Human Figure Bowl (Ruby Creek)

51
Seated Human Figure Bowl (Lytton)

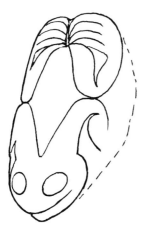

52

Seated Human Figure Bowl with Frog (Lytton)

Art is for thinking as well as seeing. Upright, this sculptured equation shows a flat-bottomed, inefficient "bowl", with a knurled rim. Upside-down, it shows a flat-bottomed, inefficient "bowl", with a knurled rim. Are they somehow referring to the same "bowl"? Upright, it is a human, with a drilled anal perforation, holding the bowl between its arms and legs.

The hands with which she lifts the frog to her own frog-like mouth . . . are the hind feet of the frog. That frog is lifting itself. Frog's hands are also her hind feet. What neither of them can see is that each is the other. What she cannot seem to see is that she is about to consume herself. She weeps, and her tears fall in the form of human beings.

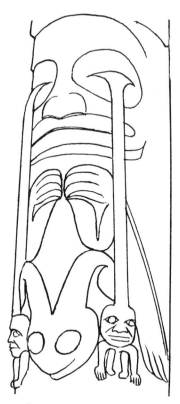

"Volcano Woman, on totem pole, shedding long tears." (Barbeau, Haida Myths, Fig. 19)

Upside-down, it is a frog, with a drilled anal perforation, holding the bowl between its legs and arms. Are they somehow the same? Where have I seen a similar equation of frog and human? On Edenshaw's tobacco mortar from Kiusta /No. 127/? And on the Haida totem pole at the Provincial Museum which we call the Weeping Woman of Tanoo? Is this the same Frog as on /No. 124/?

53
Seated Human Figure Bowl (Lytton)

Rattlesnake brow, toad on the back, but what is the face on
the front of the bowl? That which they share with the human?

54
Seated Human Figure Bowl (Lytton)

55
Seated Human Figure Bowl (Lytton)

56
Seated Human Figure Bowl (Lillooet)

57
Seated Human Figure Bowl (Kamloops)

"Said by the Indians to have been used in puberty ceremonies. The sitting figure is supposed to represent a woman giving birth to a child. The depression held the sacred water with which the shaman sprinkled the girl on her return from retirement in the woods." (Charles Hill-Tout)

58
Sawn Nephrite

The saw was made of grains of sand, and time.

59
Nephrite Blade

60

Bird: Spear-thrower Weight

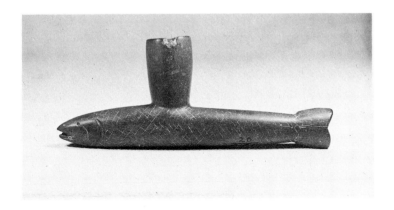

61

Smoking Pipe: Fish (Lytton)

In ancient times, pipe-smoking in America extended north and west as far as Lytton, but not to the northern coast, where the Haida tobacco was chewed.

62

Bear (Kamloops)

63

Bear (Kamloops)

64

Eagle

65

Man (Metlakatla)

66

Phalliform Man (Bella Coola)

A pun for fun, the part that is the whole.

67
Mother and Child (Bella Bella)

68

"Stone Marker" (Nass River)

Not an image of a life-form, nor an image of man, nor an image of its use, it is nonetheless "on purpose". What purpose? Perhaps just to express relationships or measurements.

69

Charm: The Eye-Hand Combination

A hand with two thumbs is, in a sense, both hands at the same time. An eye in such a hand, it follows, is both eyes. Perhaps the maker of this charm could see it both ways.

70

Hand Hammer (Basic Type)

If female sexual symbolism is the unifying concept in the images of "fonts of life" and "vessels of thought", male symbolism is the unifying concept in the "images of power". It is almost as though both concepts are derived from the ancient partnership of the mortar and the pestle; the one vulvic, the other phallic. This imagery seems to run through the entire evolution of the forms, partly as artistic play with the binary

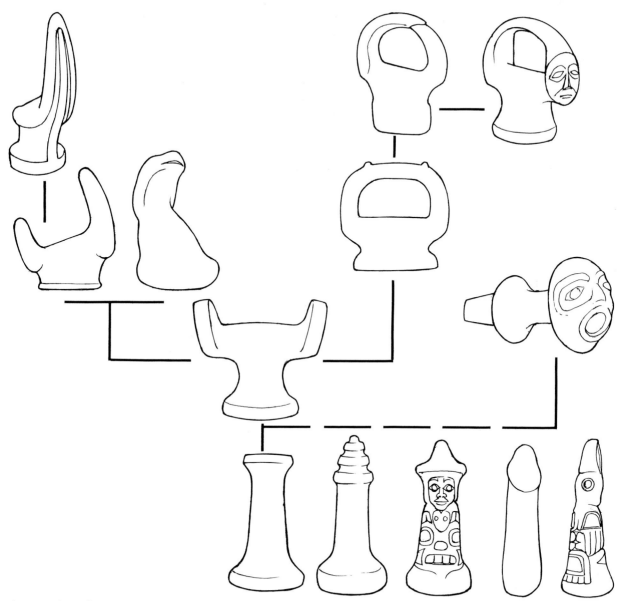

Conceptual evolution of types of Northwest Coast hand hammers. The basic type seems to have originated in the south from an ancestral form of pestle. On the northern coast, the beautifully-sculptured T-shaped, stirrup-handled, and slope-handled types evolved. Without losing their utility as hammers, they also became images of sexual duality and equations in logic.

opposition of sex, but also as general equations in logic, either in the abstract or in reference to the fundamental binary opposition of life and death.

The basic type of Northwest Coast hand hammer, which is usually described as being like "an old-fashioned telephone receiver", is at least twenty centuries old in the south, at the mouth of the Fraser River. It was like a pestle in form, with a nipple top /No. 71/. Along the Fraser Valley there was much elaboration of the nipple tops /No. 72/, but it finally became more uniformly the flat-topped variety /No. 70/, which spread in smaller numbers up the coast and provided the base from which the more complex forms evolved.

The basic type, while first and foremost an effective hammer for driving chisels and wedges, is also a pleasing sculptural form whose shape speaks clearly of its use. In the male hand, it is not difficult to imagine why it took on the phallic metaphor. Its gently-tapered shaft feels pleasurable in use, as the rhythmic jolts of pounding cause the half-relaxed grip to tighten on each impact. Such imagery finds confirmation in the examples which are explicitly phalliform, and lay bare the thrust of the thought at play /Nos. 74, 75/. In most cases, however, the sexual image was phallic rather than phalliform, metaphoric rather than explicit. The hammer that is also a little man with a hat /No. 76/, and the tobacco pestle which is also beaky Raven himself /No. 77/, may perhaps be seen in that light.

The evolution of the T-shaped, "stirrup", and slope-handled types occurred on the northern coast, in what seems to have been a burst of creative experimentation. The implement did not lose its practical function of being a hammer (except for No. 82 which is a work of pure sculpture); in fact it improved, to protect the hand, and fit the grip more comfortably, and carry its weight less awkwardly. The handle seems first to have been turned at right angles, creating the T-shaped maul. Then two lines of thought were followed, which created the stirrup and slope-handled types. Our concern is not so much with the hammers themselves as with the self images they display, the metaphorical statements of what else it is they are also about. What is being suggested is that they continued to play with the sexual metaphor, and, in that guise, with the very logic of such binary oppositions. In the light of other recent studies of Northwest Coast art and myth, it is not at all a strange suggestion. The turning of the handle at right angles to create the T-shaped maul must have been profoundly satisfying to the mind as well as the hand, because it created two typical Northwest Coast paradoxes: a thing that is also its opposite, and one thing that is also two. The completion of the stirrup handle to encircle the hand must also have been satisfying, because it created another typical reciprocal pair, the grasper-grasped; the sexual implications of which are perhaps better imagined than described.

On the T-shaped maul, the "cross" of the T has two ends, which were usually shown deliberately as being exactly the same /No. 78/. Even when the stirrup is completed, this bilateral symmetry is usually maintained, as on No. 80, where the two ends have identical faces. This equation is a basic melody upon which variations can be played, while keeping the melody in mind. Such is No. 81, where one of the ends seems to be "eating" the other, although they both start being the same. There is a slight slope to the hand-grip as well, and perhaps these two measured departures from the basic symmetry of the melody form another gentle equation.

The most subtle effects, however, were obtained on the slope-handled mauls /Nos. 82, 83/. If turning the hand-hold at right angles creates an opposite and the paradox "both at the same time", turning it 45 degrees creates an even more subtle paradox: "both and neither at the same time". On No. 82, the fine abstract sculpture which has risen through this conceptual evolution of hammers to become a pure image of what else it is they are also about, the hand-grip has become a "neither that is both": phallic above, vulvic below. And that does not exhaust its meaning as a logical equation, for the melody of "both ends the same" lingers on. Seen that way, the one end is the phallo-vulvic "neither that is both", the other end, left blank, is an implied question. What *is* the bilateral opposite of that state of affairs? As a sexual joke, the question is perhaps being rephrased in the gentle, sensuous, head-like image of No. 83, which can find nothing to eat but herself. But as a general question in logic (what is the opposite of that which is neither and both at the same time?) it has a configuration which we seem to encounter elsewhere: as Frog's problem, as the problem of the twin stone masks, and perhaps as the problem of understanding "black holes" in our own space.

71
Pestle

72
Hand Hammer: Nippletop

73
Hand Hammer (Zoomorphic Maul)

74

Hand Hammer: Phalliform

Reduced to natural size.

75

Phalliform Pestle

Reduced to natural size.

76

Hand Hammer: Man with Hat

77

Tobacco Pestle: Raven

78

Hand Hammer (T-shaped Maul)

Physically and conceptually, the T-shaped maul is a profoundly satisfying study of balance, reminiscent of the form of No. 6.

79

Hand Hammer (Stirrup Maul)

80
Hand Hammer (Stirrup Maul)

81
Hand Hammer (Stirrup Maul)

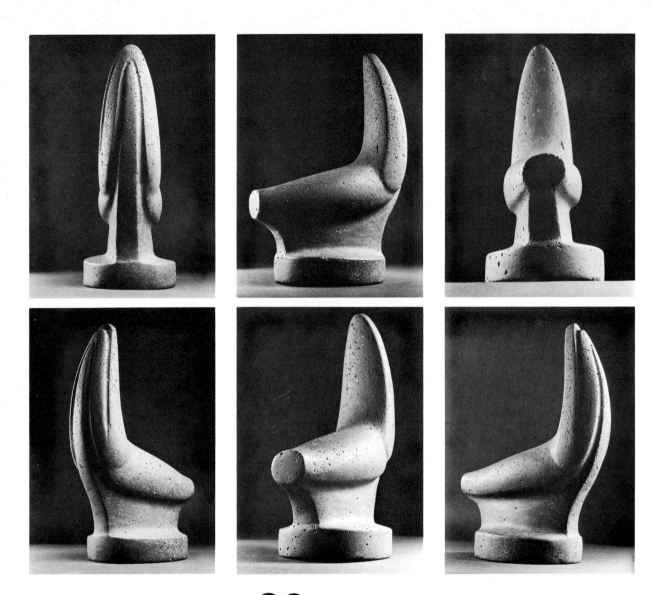

82

Hand Hammer (Slope-handled Maul)

The evolving images of hand hammers reach their culmination in this piece of pure abstract sculpture, which was not meant for actual use as a hammer.

83

Hand Hammer (Slope-handled Maul)

84

Slave Killer

This symbolic weapon may be seen as part of the conceptual evolution of hand hammers. To the basic type of hammer /No. 70/, has been added a chisel-like bit, creating the paradox of the hammer head that is also a hilt. This calls into necessity the image on the top, an equal and opposite paradox: life's face hungry for death (or the reverse), or the mouth that is also an eye /No. 88/.

This image of death is so powerful that wooden simulations were worn as part of their costume by Kwakiutl dancers in certain of their winter rituals.

85
Slave Killer

86
Slave Killer

87
Head of Slave Killer

88
Head of Slave Killer

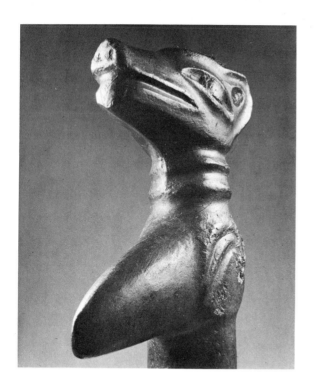

89
Slave Killer or Club

Images of Power: Sledge Hammers

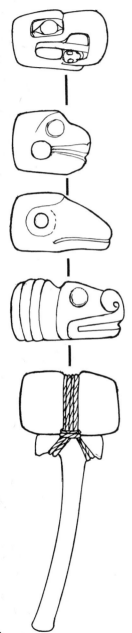

90

Sledge Hammer:
The "Hawk" that Eats Whales

Hafted mauls or sledge hammers were made by the people of the northern coast and used for pounding wedges, chisels, and stakes for fish weirs. Their images are punned animal heads, more often generic than specific. The metaphor is therefore "head" and "striker". The crowning image of the series is that of a Haida "Thunderbird" with a whale in the curve of its beak. This bird, more often called "hawk", occurs too frequently in Northwest Coast art to be explained away as a crest, and seems to be a symbol of a process: the act of intertransformation, shown as between bird and man. On a sledge hammer, what it wields symbolically is "transformation".

105

91
Sledge Hammer Head

92

Sledge Hammer Head

93

Sledge Hammer Head

94

Sledge Hammer Head

95

Sledge Hammer

96
Sledge Hammer Head: Raven Alighting

97

Pile Driver: Shark Head

Salmon weirs were built across streams by the people of the northern and central coast, by pounding pointed stakes into the stream-bed with two-handed, heavy strikers. The crowning image of the pile driver is this shark head, a crest of the Eagle clan. The thumbs fit into the "eyes"; the rest of the fingers, on the other side, into "gill slits". The scowling, fearsome mouth of the shark has an indication of a labret. Shark-Woman's mouth, phallic outline: another equation of opposites.

98
Pile Driver: Circular Face

99
Pile Driver

100
Pile Driver: Man with Headache

Images of Power:
Death-Bringers (Clubs)

101
Club

In 1898, in the upper Skeena country, Johnny Muldoe was digging a hole for a house-post on the flat just below the Hagwilget Canyon of the Bulkley River, and four feet down, under a capping stone, he found 35 stone clubs cached together. He handed them over to Mr. A. W. Vowell, Superintendent of Indian Affairs for British Columbia, who happened to be visiting Hazelton at the time, and they became part of Mr. Vowell's private collection in Victoria. Dr. C. F. Newcombe photographed them and made notes which were the basis for an article in the Annual Report of the Provincial Museum for 1962 (Duff, 1963), and Mr. Vowell gave him one, which went with the Newcombe Collection to the museum /No. 102/. The rest were presumably acquired by the collector G. T. Emmons, and some of them, at least, found their way into the Museum of the American Indian in New York /Nos. 101, 103, 104/. The clubs from the Hagwilget cache, and others from the same vicinity which are in the same style, are among the most singular images from our thirty centuries of stone sculpture. The rest of the clubs in the exhibit are from widely scattered locations along the coast.

One of the most curious things about the stone clubs is that they are not so much functional weapons as they are images of weapons. They are either stone replicas of functional clubs, or metaphors in stone of what "club" might also mean. When ordinary weapons were required, clubs of wood, antler, and bone were presumably preferred. Sometimes, judging from the images, these were inset with stone striking blades. Stone, that is to say, was really more important as a medium for metaphoric messages than as a material for practical weapons. Needless to say, the imagery, often as not, is phallic.

Tsimshian myths make the occasional mention of stone clubs, and these are usually magic clubs. They are capable, for example, of killing enemies by turning their entire villages upside down. Another tradition of the Hazelton area may be a clue to the Hagwilget cache. It tells of an old woman who gathered up the weapons of the slain after a war and cached them away, and then was killed herself. The tradition may link the cache to the Gitksan people of Hazelton, however the style of the clubs is archaic, in that it bears little resemblance to the style of Northwest Coast art as known in historic times.

Apart from those which are replicas in stone of wooden or antler prototypes, or are long pestles adapted for striking rather

116

than grinding, the sculptured stone clubs seem better described as emblems than as weapons. Some of them carry images of birds, which seem identifiable as owls, kingfishers, or sandhill cranes, and these may have represented crests or guardian spirits of their owners. But the most persistent visual metaphor is that of male sexual power, and it is not, perhaps, inappropriate as a symbol of man's most potent 'weapon'.

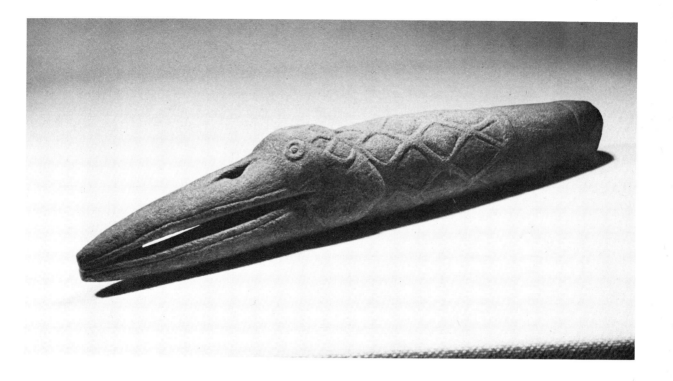

102
Club from Hagwilget Cache (Sandhill Crane)

103
Club from Hagwilget Cache (Surf Scoter)

104
Club from Hagwilget Cache (Bi-phallic)

119

105

Club: Death-Bringer

It is difficult to imagine any more perfect sculptural control of stone than this masterful club. The blade, in the shape of a Roman sword, is in this case a lethal weapon. The handle, bearing its unique head, may also be a message of death. It is just that the whole sculpture is so perfect that it gives the lie to its message by vibrating with life.

106
Club

107
Club: "Kingfisher"

108
Club: "Fish"

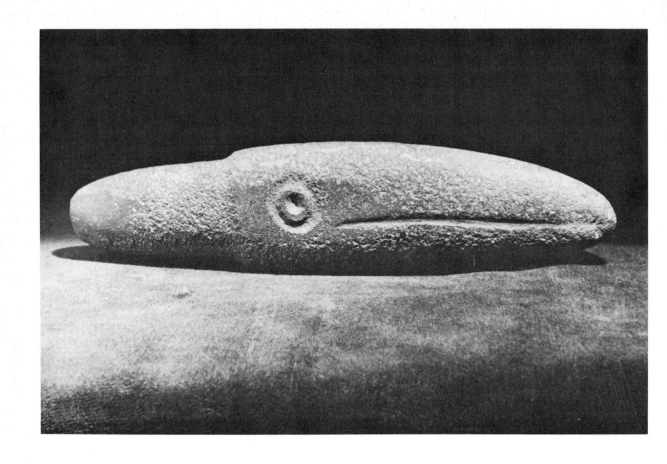

109

Club: Self-Eating Mouth

If viewed as a set of relationships, this club can be described as a mouth capable of swallowing itself. The same applies to Nos. 107 and 108, and to the "Frog" tobacco mortars.

110
Club

111
Club: "Bird"

112 Club (Quadra Island)

113 Club (Powell River)

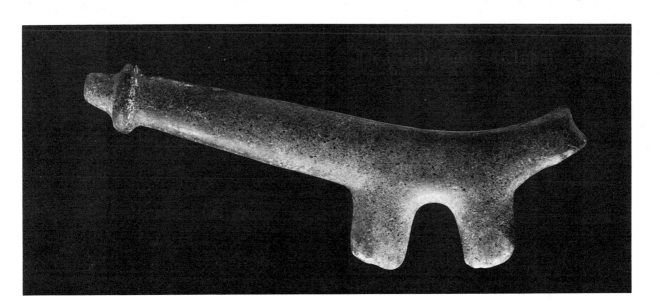

114
Club (Burrard Inlet)

Vessels of Thought: Paint Dishes

115

Paint Dish

The top is a face, the bottom a body. The dish is therefore a mouth and a belly at the same time.

116
Paint Dish: Frog

117
Paint Dish

118
Paint Dish

Vessels of Thought:
Tobacco Mortars

George M. Dawson, the famous Canadian geologist, wrote a report on the Queen Charlotte Islands and their Haida inhabitants in 1878, in which he included references to the single plant which in pre-white times they had cultivated in gardens, an isolated species of the narcotic American weed, tobacco. Paradoxically, by that time, they had abandoned the custom of chewing their home-grown variety, and had adopted from the white man the custom of smoking commercial tobacco in pipes. In 1878 the only tobacco patch left on the Charlottes was tended by an old woman of Cumshewa, whom Dawson was not able to visit. He wrote:

The Haidas used to grow it not only for themselves, but as an article of trade with other neighbouring tribes. To prepare the plant for use it was dried over the fire on a little framework, finely bruised in a stone mortar, and then pressed into cakes. It was not smoked in a pipe, but being mixed with a little lime prepared by burning clam-shells, was chewed or held in the cheek. The stone mortars . . . are still to be found stowed away in the corners of the houses . . .

The stone mortars already mentioned as having been employed in the preparation of the native tobacco, now seem to be little if at all used for any purpose. They are generally circular in outline and without ornamentation, being in some cases very roughly made. Other examples are ornamented by carving. (Dawson, 1880, pp. 115, 141)

Dawson collected three of those which are "ornamented by carving", and which he perhaps found "stowed away in the corners of the houses"; these are among the images shown in this exhibition /Nos. 121, 123, 127/.

In "A Review of the Northwest Coast Tobacco Mystery" (*Syesis*, 5: 249-257, 1972), Nancy Turner and Roy Taylor have summarized what is known about the Haida tobacco. It was also grown and chewed by the Tlingit people, who acquired their seeds from the Haida; and judging from the distribution of the mortars, it may have been chewed by some of the Tsimshian people as well. How it got to the northern coast is not known. Its closest cousin was found in the Lytton area, and was not chewed but smoked in stone pipes /No. 61/. The antiquity of Haida tobacco is also unknown. The mortars, quite unlike the seated human figure bowls of the south, have not been found in circumstances that suggest great age; and the art style which they exhibit is the mature and fully-developed style of the northern Northwest Coast into historic times. These northern vessels evolved later than the southern fonts of life, and their time ended with the extinction of the Haida tobacco in the 1880s.

If we had a better knowledge of the occasions upon which the Haida people chewed their tobacco, we would have a better idea of its meanings in their culture and their thought. There is no reason, however, to project our own hapless image of tobacco use, that of the chain-smoker, onto them. Judging from their later use of pipes, tobacco was reserved largely for important ritual occasions, like funerals and house-buildings. In a culture without peyote, or alcohol, or cannabis, or aspirin, it was the principal narcotic and mind-bending drug. I suggest that its principal occasions may have been those that had something of the idea of "smoking the pipe of peace": occasions of meetings of minds, of emerging consensuses, of decision-making.

In symbolic terms, that tobacco would fall into a strange and ambiguous category: food but not food; not food but not poison either; its narcotic effect as aptly considered a taste of death as an extra helping of life. We say that we "chew nails and spit out spikes". Perhaps the Haida "chewed ambiguities and spit out consensuses".

Our concern is not so much with the tobacco itself, but with the images which the mortars proclaim, and the meanings of those images. Here as elsewhere we can be satisfied by an easy answer if we choose: they simply represent crests of the owner. But the simple answer does not explain the complex structure of the images, which seems to be a symptom of a deeper interplay of meaning, beneath the guise of crests.

Sexual symbolism, I suggest, is not the underlying theme of these vessels of thought. Such a conclusion is a strange one to reach, considering that the mortar and pestle is such an ancient and obvious model of the sexual duality. The mortar in the form of a seal dish, No. 130, does have an echo of the vulvic form, but its head seems strangely ambiguous. The pestle used for grinding tobacco, No. 77, is indeed in some sense phallic, but is also in the form of Mr. Paradox of Haida myth, Raven himself. The underlying theme, I suggest, is the more generalized one of "transformation". A tobacco mortar was a mixing bowl out of which emerged the essential ingredient of decision. What I think the images are trying to reflect is the discovery of the common ground of meaning, the emergence of the elusive common ground of consensus.

Beaver Mortars

119
Tobacco Mortar: Beaver

We can make a start with the three mortars showing Beaver and his hands, which may all be by the same artist.

On the first, the incisor teeth and flat tail symbolize Beaver, a well-known crest of the Eagle clan of the Haida. What is unusual is the manner in which Beaver is applied to the mortar. His hands are human hands, and are shown backwards, as though they are the ones holding up the mortar to look at its face. On the back, the tail of Beaver, upside down and mask-like, is a human face. It is as though Man holds up the mortar as a mirror, and "sees" that he is wearing a Beaver mask.

120
Tobacco Mortar: Beaver

On the second mortar, Beaver's hands are yet more compli-
cated. On the front, they hold his chewing stick, a symbol
of his identity and the food out of which he reconstitutes
himself as Beaver. But those strange little hands come out of
his cheeks, not his body, and that strange little stick is wholly

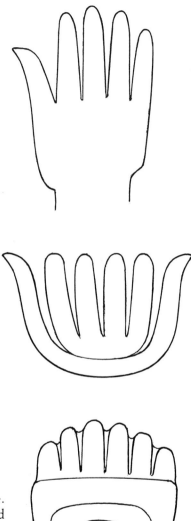

inside his mouth, as though he were taking an inside bite. Larger hands reach around to the back of the mortar, and hold a human face or mask, which is also the Beaver's tail. One of these hands is twice as big as the other. All of the hands are very strange hands: two-thumbed hands, both-ways hands, like the one on the little hand-eye charm, No. 69. The same strange hands that in front have equal holds upon the chewing stick, on the back have unequal holds upon the human mask. This Beaver's hands "hold it both ways". This Beaver's food is human masks.

137

121

Tobacco Mortar: "Frog and Man"

The third mortar seems to be working on the same problem, trying to bring Frog into the equation.

The first mortar is recognizing itself as one of man's masks. The second is feeding itself on man's masks. Man chews tobacco, and sees his masks dissolve.

122

Tobacco Mortar: Frog with Eyebrows

We come now to the image of Frog. Frog was fairly common as a "crest". Knowing that, we are not under any necessity to seek out deeper meanings. And yet, he sometimes seems to have a very strange mouth, very strange eyes.

123

Tobacco Mortar: Frog with Eyebrows

The mouth of "Frog With Eyebrows" — twice repeated, perhaps by the same artist — is really a very large mouth. Set into action, is it meant as being big enough to swallow the whole mortar? Strange question. Another way to put it, no more strange: Has he just done so? Follow Frog's eyebrows, they become Frog's forelegs. How's that again? A pun, a mental trick, but it turns eyes into shoulders, head into body, part into whole, swallower into swallowed, "about to be swallowed" and "has just swallowed", neither and both, at the same time. Is that why he looks so self-satisfied? Or she?

124

Tobacco Mortar: Frog of Beauty

If Frog can be beautiful, this is a beautiful Frog: such perfect lines, so round and plump, so full a mouth. Those eyes, so large, and wide, and open; they must be both-seeing eyes. But isn't Frog supposed to be "neither" as well as "both"? Not this one. At least she doesn't seem to think so.

125

Tobacco Mortar: Frog (Unfinished)

Two Frog mortars with eyes unopened. Is it just coincidence, or is this Frog with neither-seeing eyes? The second mortar has Frog and "hawk" in equal stages of emergence at either end, and Frog has hints of feathers at the elbows. These may be two equally good ways of saying the same thing, although neither can see it quite yet.

126
Mortar: Frog and Hawk (Unfinished?)

143

127

Tobacco Mortar: Frog and Human

This masterpiece of mortars, collected by Dawson in the summer of 1878 from Edenshaw's village of Kiusta (then twenty years deserted), can be seen simply as a representation of Frog, one of Edenshaw's favourite crests. But to see only that would be like seeing only the literal meaning of a proverb. The mortar is a multiple pun, and Edenshaw's Frog crest, as we know from other representations, such as his "chief's seat" in the Provincial Museum, is more than a simple meta-

phor. As a starting point, consider that the Frog's wide, wide mouth has just snapped shut. It has just done what Frog with Eyebrows is shown about to do, with results that we can see. The human figure at the other end, for all the world like a seated human figure bowl, wears the mouth of the bowl as her labret perforation, and therefore must be female. Her arms extend along the rim. Or are they Frog's legs? Or both? At any rate, the human figure has just been swallowed whole. Behind Frog's mouth is a flipper; she is also being punned as seal. She also has strange eyes. This masterpiece of mortars reveals the concepts which link the mortars and seal dishes of the north with the seated human figure bowls, much more ancient, of the south; and suggests the sequence of ideas by which Frog ascended to her place as a symbol of pure logic.

145

A Circle of Vessels

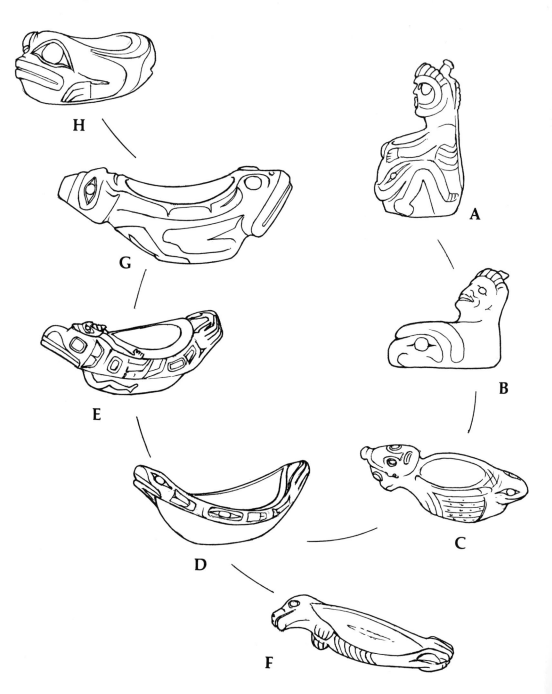

H

G

E

D

F

A

B

C

Threads of continuity, of structure and of symbol, run through the entire series of vessels, more ancient and less, that culminated in Edenshaw's Frog mortar. The unifying concept is that of female sexual symbolism. Its metaphors are woman, rattlesnake, monster, seal, and Frog. Its logic is that of the paradox of the part that contains its whole. It was of course no idle exercise in logic, for the images were applied to sacred vessels: fonts of life, dealing with the paradox that is woman, and vessels of thought, dealing with the paradox that is the human condition. Its crowning image, strange as it may seem, is the Haida Frog, which seems to have risen through the system into the realm of pure logic as the very image of ambiguity: that which is in every respect neither and both at the same time.

Bowl A in the diagram is the ancient seated human figure bowl, adorned with rattlesnakes, which was found in a Victoria rose garden /No. 30/. Its doubly-negative metaphor of rattlesnake-vulva has already been sufficiently discussed. On Bowl B, from Courtenay /No. 38/, the place of the rattlesnake has been taken by a monstrous face which cannot be identified, but which seems to convey hints of both beak and nose, bird and human, relating it to one of the most compelling images of Northwest Coast art, sometimes called "hawk". On Bowl C, an ancient, complex, human- and animal-form vessel from Langley Prairie in the Fraser Valley (Duff, 1956a, pp. 30-31, P1. 8; now in the Denver Art Museum), the human figure is reduced in size and reclines on her back, arms along the rim, with a snake's head at the other end. In addition, the entire bowl is punned as a bird, perhaps owl, back to back with the human figure.

Two wooden vessels are now introduced into the sequence to fill conceptual gaps. These are dishes in the form of a seal, used on the northern coast in historic times as "grease dishes", roughly the equivalent of our "gravy bowls". These remind us too that what we have to work with in the north is the stone art within its full context of wood and other media, while all we have in the south is the imperishable stone component. Bowl D is a typical, simple, vulviform seal dish (Smithsonian Institution, No. 23410; illustrated in *Boxes and Bowls*, 1973, Fig. 4). Bowl E is a little masterpiece on which the artist has made the meaning more visible (Smithsonian Institution, No. 89132, collected at Skidegate; illustrated in *Boxes and Bowls*, Fig. 13). A little human figure has been added — the whole has been restored to the part — with arms along the rim as on C, and legs around the bowl as on A; the whole being a seal in the sense that C is an owl. The seal's hind flippers are also punned as hands, echoing the little hands on the rim, and suggesting a manner in which the vessel might actually be held. With Bowl F we are back to prehistoric times in the Fraser Valley /No. 28/. This five-inch vulviform seal may therefore be considered as the grandmother of the seal dishes, revealing that the metaphor, vulva-seal, has some considerable antiquity.

With the Kiusta Frog mortar, Bowl G, the threads come finally together. It is a Frog mortar, seal dish, and seated human figure bowl, all at the same time. The reason is that all are really about the same thing. That thing is made of the stuff of analogy, it is that which is common to the mouth, where eating occurs, the belly, where digestion and gestation occur, and the vulva, where life-giving occurs. What the mortar is full of, therefore, is creative transformation. And Frog turns out to be more than seal, more than a simple metaphor for vulva. In creating Frog, the logic doubles back upon itself. Frog's mouth is so big that it can swallow even the vessel it adorns; in fact, has just done so, has just done what the Weeping Woman on the Tanoo totem pole is shown just about to do. Frog is not all the terrifying double-negative logic of the rattle-snake-vulva. As we have seen in the Salish myth, that concept calls into necessity the death-defying bi-pointed stick, the death-dealing bi-phallic club. Frog opts for the different opposite: the comforting, self-reversing double-negative of having it both ways. Frog has need for neither tooth nor beak. There is no place in Frog's system for death. Frog sees the need only for mothers, not fathers. Frog rises through sexual symbolism to emerge, alive and well, a creature of pure logic: the self-swallowing mouth and its opposite, the self-swallowing mouth; 50-50, both and neither at the same time. In the Frog mortars, the circle of stone vessels aspires to become a helix of eternal life. Which may explain why She looks so perfectly smug on Bowl H /No. 124/.

This is not the place to delve further into the role into which Frog had ascended in the art and logic of the northern coast by historic times. A crest, but something more as well, it had become one of the main actors in a system of logical paradoxes, the exploration of which was one of the most active hidden agendas of the art. Frog became — or so it seems to me — a convenient and friendly opposite-sign; part sublime but part absurd; at the same time a serious attempt to be neither and both at once, and a knowing reminder that you can't really have it both ways, as she seems to think. The opposite of everything else, without being zero or death, she was therefore a symbol of life pure and simple.

128

Tobacco Mortar: Grinning Bear

One of the best-kept secrets of Northwest Coast art is that most of the bears wear wide, not to say fatuous grins. Frog wears a wry, Mona Lisa kind of smile, but bear simply grins. Elsewhere in the art, grinning faces are hard to find. The funny thing about bear is that he seems to be grinning in contexts that imply his own demise. The joke, that is to say, seems to be on him. The grin should really be on the other side of his face. This little bowl is a bear grinning with every ounce of his being,

on his face and in body-language. What's the joke? Maybe it
is let out of the bag by the wooden dish which seems to be
about exactly the same thing. That bear's own rear end is
that of a beaver, and it is wearing exactly the same all over
grin.

Wooden oil dish in the shape of bear. From an early collection. Illustrated in Seibert and Forman, 1967, Pl. 64.

129

Tobacco Mortar: Bear (Unfinished?)

Two faces are emerging from the opposite ends of this happy mortar too, but it is not yet clear what they are.

130

Tobacco Mortar: Seal

Tobacco mortar made in the image of a seal dish. The large
mouth seems reminiscent of Frog.

131

Tobacco Mortar: Raven

One of the prime objects of Northwest Coast art is the famous "Raven rattle" used by northern chiefs. There are hints on this sophisticated Raven mortar that it has similar meanings, expressed in the equation of the tobacco mortar. The projection on the throat suggests the recurved beak of the "hawk" on the

breast of the rattle (and on the tail of the wooden dish, which seems to be another variation on the Raven rattle theme). The wings on the mortar are also punned as upside-down, profile faces.

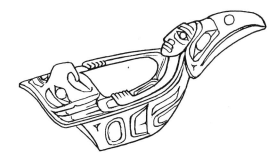

Wooden grease dish reminiscent of the Raven mortar and of the Raven rattle (Smithsonian Institution No. 178961, from Boxes and Bowls, 1973, Fig. 26)

132
Tobacco Mortar?: Emerging Raven?

133
Tobacco Mortar: Mouth

134
Tobacco Mortar: One Face, Four Times

With this great masterwork of art and thought we arrive back at Man's prime image: himself. The first thing to see is that the four faces are carefully, meticulously, one.

Most bowls, like most living things, have a front and back as opposite as head and tail, and two sides as identical as two wings or two hands. On this bowl front, back, left, right are one. That which is common to all is humanity, seeing, recognizing (as on the twin stone masks which follow). The pattern is of paradox redoubled, two opposite pairs of opposites, all one; each a mask looking, each a mirror seeing, the same. This artist had found a pattern with ancient roots in human contemplation: that of the Quaternity, that of the four faces of Brahma, that of the wheel in the air, that of Matthew, Mark, Luke, and John.

159

Image of Recognition:
The Twin Masks

135
Image of Mask

136
Image of Mask

In this matched pair of masks, the supreme masterwork of the entire exhibition, everything comes into focus in the eyes. The first thing to see is that the artist deliberately and carefully made the two the same; they are two masks of the one face. The second thing to see is that in their most vital feature, the eyes, he made them profoundly opposite. They are, with full self-consciousness, a paradox. What the paradox is about is whatever "masks" are about, and whatever "seeing" is about. They are good for thinking as well as for seeing. For example, think of one as the husband and the other the wife, or one as the mask and the other its mirror. Or think of what self-recognition really means.

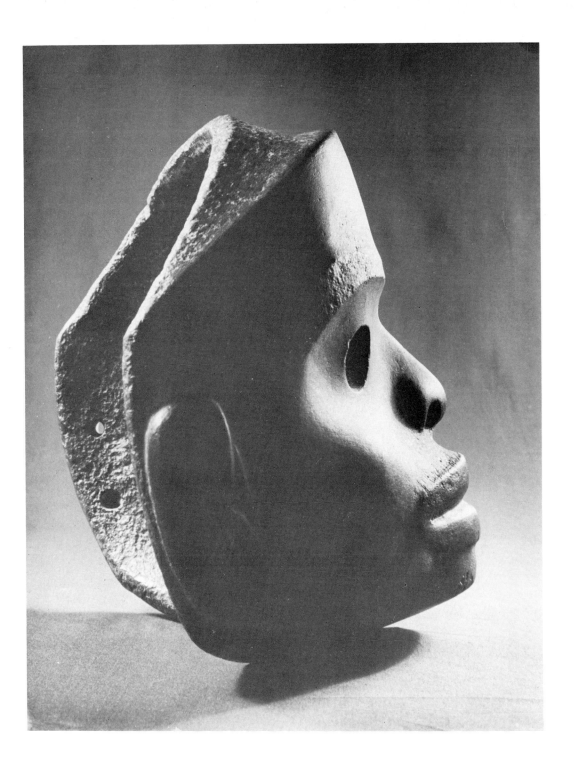

The Twin Masks

The historical facts known about the masks are few. One, the "unsighted twin", was collected at the Tsimshian village of Kitkatla in 1879 by Indian Commissioner I. W. Powell, and is treasured as a masterpiece by the National Museum of Canada in Ottawa. The other, the "sighted twin", was collected either on the Nass River or at Metlakatla, and is treasured as a masterpiece by the Musée de l'Homme in Paris. It has been recognized for some years that the two are alike, and that they seem to be the only two stone masks from the Northwest Coast. But what has not been recognized until now is that they are far more than just alike: they are the two halfs of a single work of art, the two sides of a single profound equation. They are as alike as the two halfs of a torn dollar, or the two sides of a coin. We do not know their age. We do not know the original manner of their use, except that it was indeed as "mask": the one in Paris formerly had, inside, a tooth-marked wooden harness. My best guess is that they were worn by a single performer in the winter rituals known as "halait" (sacred), and were secretly switched, in the blink of an eye, to demonstrate a kind of power that logic alone finds incredible. My guess is that they were meant to be seen on the same occasion, but not in the same glance: while the one was on open view to the eye, the other was fresh in the memory. I would not think it proper to show them to you side by side, but I did want, with passion enough to pilgrimage to Ottawa and to Paris, to bring them into each other's presence once again.

The toughness of stone yielded to the mastery of the artist two likenesses of the same visage, which may have been an idealized image of himself. But the one has eyes that have never opened, the other has eyes that can never close. The one sees only inward and backward, the other sees only outward and forward. These eyes, being of stone, are exempt from the usual alternations of mortal eyes: blinking, sleeping, closing for contemplation or for death. Think more about the open, perfect-circle eyes of the "sighted twin" from Metlakatla and Paris. It is not that they have "opened" or "wakened", for they have no lids for such a purpose. Their vision is of a purer kind, eternally open to the outside light. Now think more about the unopen eyes of the "unsighted twin" from Kitkatla and Ottawa. It is not that they have "closed" for sleep or contemplation, for they have no lids for such a purpose. Nor are they the eyes of death, for Northwest Coast artists had different ways of depicting dead eyes, and also these are eyes on a living face, the same face as the "sighted twin". It is that their kind of vision is of a purer kind, eternally open to the inner light. The Tsimshian artist has shown the two to be as alike as twins, and as separate: outer vision and inner vision, sight and memory, seeing and imagining. He has shown the two in the act of self-recognition, both equally masks, both equally mirrors.

The culminating image of thirty centuries of stone sculpture is really about the glint of recognition, which is the purest pulse of life. Eyes of the past and eyes of the future meet and there is a thrill of recognition the instant they both see that they share an equal hint of Frog's wry smile.

EPILOGUE (January 23, 1975)

The two masks fit together!

Everything else was ready for the printer before I went to Paris to bring home the second mask, which we had seen only in the form of a single published illustration. What remained was to get it to Victoria, get it photographed, and the catalogue would be complete. But what we had not foreseen, so skilfully had the artist created his illusion, was the astonishing truth that the two nest snugly together. The slightly more delicate face of the "sighted twin" from Paris and Metlakatla fits tightly inside the "unsighted twin" from Ottawa and Kitkatla. No more perfect a consummation could possibly have been imagined.

While the implications of this discovery have not fully sunk in, I see no need to change anything said or implied earlier about this great masterwork of visual thought, except to suggest that we can now make a better guess about the manner in which it was worn. The inner mask is the one with drilled perforations on top, bottom, and sides (ears) for the wooden harness which most likely rested over the head and was steadied by the teeth. The outer mask has only the top perforations, and it may be suggested that it was held in the hands, and was fitted into place by sighting through the eye-holes to the targets behind its eyes. It probably goes too far to suggest that the wearer might have supported the nested pair without using his hands. I still suggest that they were not shown side by side, but dramatically alternated to the audience's view.

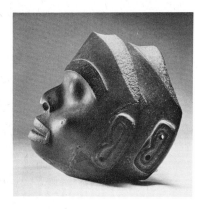

The theatrical effect must have been a marvel, as the dancer turned and those stone eyes "closed". But still more of a marvel is the total conception of the artist, and it seems to me that everything I suggested earlier about his mature contemplation of the matched paradoxes of "seeing" and "masking" is now confirmed and reinforced. What a masterpiece of illusion! The two faces are the same, in total size, in visage, in expression (and even in the scratches on the forehead); yet one fits within the other. The two sets of eyes are opposite, and that circumstance was used in fitting the two together. Both have equal hints of parentage of Frog, which perhaps was the secret to "see", for in that recognition was the deepest of the meanings. They are about seeing and masking. They are about self-recognition. I cannot help but think that if they could speak, their message would be what Raven's grandfather said to Raven in one of the Haida creation myths: "I am you. That is you". And as Hilary keeps saying, what boggles the mind is that he made them of stone.

catalogue

1
The "Sechelt Image"

Height: 20"
Centennial Museum, Vancouver, B.C.
QAA-2036

Found at Sechelt about 1921. Weight: 70 lbs. References: Foster, 1926, p. 14; Duff, 1956a, P1. 22c and p. 88. Here interpreted as a strength-testing stone, the image restating "strength" in the metaphor of sex.

Strength-testing stones are known from a small number of Kwakiutl and Salish villages. I am informed by Peter Macnair that Kwakiutl marriage festivities sometimes included the lifting of a greased strength-stone by the groom.

2
Animal Form: The Most Ancient Known Image

Length: 2¼"
Museum of Anthropology, University of B.C.
DjRi3: 5657

Excavated from the Milliken Site near Yale, this steatite carving shows a mouth, round eyes, backbone, ribs, and feet. It is attributed by Dr. C. E. Borden to the Baldwin Phase, dating from about 900 B.C. He suggests that the 3000-year old image represents a seal, and it shows the wear of much handling.

3
Spindle Whorl: Snakes and Eyes

Diameter: 4½"
Museum of Anthropology, University of B.C.
DjRi3: 11142

Found at the Milliken Site in the Fraser Canyon above Yale, this elaborately carved whorl is attributed by Dr. C. E. Borden to the Emery Phase, dating from about 800 A.D. Steatite. The convex side shows an incipient human face in a sea of eyes, the spindle hole also being an eye. On the reverse, three coiled snakes are surrounded by eyes.

4
Double Labret

Length: 2¾"
Museum of Anthropology, University of B.C.
DhRt 6:1401

Found at Locarno Beach, and probably associated with the Locarno Beach Phase, about 2000 years old. Labrets were ornaments worn through perforations in the lower lip. This one is here interpreted as an abstract sculpture restating an essential meaning of the labret.

5
Labret with Appendage

Length: 2"
Centennial Museum, Vancouver, B.C.
QAA-922

Worn in the lower lip, only the central button and appendage would be visible. Found at Point Gray, Vancouver.

6
Pure Form

Greatest dimension: 1 9/16"
Mrs. W. H. Cross,
Sidney, B.C.

Found by Mrs. Cross weathered out of the bank at a well-known archaeological site on the Gulf Islands, this superb little soapstone sculpture is the masterpiece of the archaeological puzzles known as the "Gulf Islands complex", or "whatsits" (Duff, 1956b; Duff, 1956a, p. 83; Mitchell, 1971, pp. 114-117). The use and meaning of these small artifacts, of which there are several types, are not known. Their age is about 2500 years.

7
Hunchback Man

Height: 16"
National Museum of Man, Ottawa
XII-B-1563

Found on an archaeological site between Ladner and Boundary Bay, collected by Harlan I. Smith in 1923. Sandstone. Use unknown. Reference: Duff, 1956a, p. 89, Pl. 22b.

8
Human Figure

Height: 13"
National Museum of Man, Ottawa
XII-B-1488

Found at what is probably the same site as the previous figure, this upright sandstone image is

badly weathered. Collected by Harlan I. Smith. Use unknown. Reference: Duff, 1956a, p. 89, Pl. 22a.

9
Head

Height: 6½"
Centennial Museum, Vancouver, B.C.
QAA-386

No data.

10
Head

Height: 3"
Mission District Historical Society, Mission City, B.C.
1972-1-62

Found at Hatzic Lake in the Fraser Valley. Reference: Duff, 1956a, p. 80, Pl. 20e.

11
Head

Height: 4½"
Langley Centennial Museum, Fort Langley, B.C.
58-18-1

Broken from some larger figure, this soapstone head was ploughed up near Langley in 1923.

12
Face

Diameter: 2"
Provincial Museum, Victoria, B.C.
ER-y-835

Found between Lytton and Lillooet.

13
Crouching Man

Length: 1¾"
Simon Fraser University Museum of Anthropology
and Archaeology
DiRi:38-1823-74

Excavated by Henning VonKrogh at Hope on the
Fraser River, this tiny figure has an expressive face
which is very difficult to see, but worth the effort.

14
Head with "Beard"

Height: 2¼"
Centennial Museum, Vancouver, B.C.
QAD-1416

Found at Boston Bar on the Fraser River, this strange
face is made of an undetermined kind of red stone.
Reference: Duff, 1956a, p. 80, Pl. 20f.

15
Animal-form Bowl

Length: 10"
Centennial Museum, Vancouver, B.C.
QAA-1085

Quatsino Sound. Reference: Duff, 1956a, p. 61, Pl.
17d (said to be from Yale).

16
Paint Mortar: "Diving Porpoise"

Length: 8½"
Provincial Museum, Victoria
618

North Arm of Fraser River (probably Marpole site).
See Duff, 1956a, p. 63 "diving porpoise"; Smith,
1903, Fig. 54b.

17
Animal-form Bowl

Length: 7"
Langley Centennial Museum, Fort Langley, B.C.
58-5-1

Ploughed up at Milner in 1931.

18
Animal-form Bowl

Length: 12"
Centennial Museum, Vancouver, B.C.
QAA-1084

Found near Bear Creek, Fraser Valley. Heads at
both ends. Reference: Duff, 1956a, p. 63, Pl. 17h.

19
Bowl: Owl

Length: 6½"
Simon Fraser University Museum of Anthropology
and Archaeology
4268

Found at the junction of the Harrison and Fraser
rivers.

20
Bowl: Bird

Length: 6½"
Centennial Museum, Vancouver, B.C.
QAA-1082

Fraser Valley.

21
Bowl: Turtle with Beetles

Length: 5"
Provincial Museum, Victoria, B.C.
3183

Bridge River, near Lillooet. See Duff, 1956a, p. 60 and Pl. 17a; Wingert, 1952, Pl. 39.

22
Bowl: Square Turtle

Length: 11½"
Langley Centennial Museum, Fort Langley, B.C.
65-9-4

This thin-walled dish is unusual in many of its features: the four markings on each side, the square shape, and the turned head of the "turtle".

23
Bowl: Twin Heads

Height: 7"
Centennial Museum, Vancouver, B.C.
QAA-1081

Said to have been found in a cave near Pemberton, this two-celled lava bowl is of unknown use and meaning. Reference: Duff, 1956a, p. 65 (Dalzell Image). It may be suggested that the heads represent salmon, which are often associated with twins in Indian belief.

24
Bowl in Head

Height: 5½"
Museum of Anthropology, University of B.C.
DgRn10:1

Found near Hatzic Lake, Fraser Valley. Reference: Duff, 1956a, p. 69, Pl. 18a.

25
Bowl in Head

Height: 8½"
National Museum of Man, Ottawa,
XII-B-1696

Found at Marpole, Vancouver. Sandstone.

26
Bowl Behind Face

Height: 17"
Museum of Anthropology, University of B.C.
A6555

Found near Sumas in the Fraser Valley, this image was broken by the plough, and mended with cement.

27
Bowl with Two Faces

Length: 3½"
Lillooet Museum, Lillooet, B.C.
73:287
Ploughed up in Lillooet in 1898.

171

28
Bowl: Vulviform Seal

Length: 5″
Centennial Museum, Vancouver, B.C.
QAA-1039

Yale, Fraser River. Here interpreted as being like northern Northwest Coast seal dishes, in having female sexual connotations. (WD)

29
Bowl, Vulviform, with Two Faces

Length: 4⅛″
Cariboo College, Kamloops, B.C.
EeR121:13-1

Excavated by Arnoud Stryd at the pit-house site EeR121 at the east end of Seton Lake near Lillooet, this little soapstone bowl is dated at about 400 A.D. It is here interpreted (WD) as a female sexual symbol, shown open on top and closed on the bottom, and it is suggested that like the seated human figure bowls it might have been used in puberty rituals.

30
Seated Human Figure Bowl with Rattlesnakes

Height: 15″
Mr. and Mrs. R. E. B. Gore-Langton, Victoria, B.C.

Dug up in a Victoria rose garden in 1960, this powerful image was associated with No. 32 and with evidence of fire. The large serpent down the back is unquestionably a rattlesnake, as is the large face on the front of the bowl. By analogy with other bowls, the cheek ridges may also be rattlesnakes. In nature, such snakes are found no closer than the Lytton area, which is also the probable source of the soapstone from which the image is made. It is one of the largest such figures.

172

31
Seated Human Figure Bowl (The Marpole Image)

Height: 10″
Centennial Museum, Vancouver
DhRs 1: 10403

This is an extremely important image because it was found during archaeological excavations in the famous Marpole midden near the mouth of the Fraser River. Its discoverer, Mr. H. Leisk, reported that it rested on the top of a stone cairn associated with a burial (Vancouver *Sun,* Sept. 8, 1934, p. 6; see also Charles Hill-Tout, *The Great Fraser Midden,* 1928). Its presence in the midden establishes its age as about 2000 years. Published in Duff, 1956a, p. 31-32. Pl. 14e. See also text for additional data from the notes on its discovery in 1930.

32
Seated Human Figure Bowl

Height: 8¾″
Mr. and Mrs. R. E. B. Gore-Langton, Victoria, B.C.

Found together with No. 30.

33
Seated Human Figure Bowl

Height: 7″ (head missing)
Museum of Anthropology, University of B.C.
A11-507c

Found at Bazan Bay, near Sidney on Vancouver Island. Human heads on front and back (main head missing). Published in Duff, 1956a, p. 36, Pl. 11.

34
Seated Human Figure Bowl

Height: 14"
Mr. John Hauberg, Seattle, Washington

Published as the Shoal Harbour Bowl in Duff, 1956a, pp. 34-35, Pl. 10, this large and complex soapstone figure was found a short distance from a shellmound at North Saanich, Vancouver Island. The large headdress depicting snakeskins and human feet is unique.

35
Seated Human Figure Bowl

Height: 6¼"
Mr. and Mrs. R. E. B. Gore-Langton, Victoria, B.C.

Found weathered out of the bank at the south end of Kuper Island in the 1950s, on the beach, at midnight, by firelight, while cooking clams.

36
Seated Human Figure Bowl

Height: 3¾"
Provincial Museum, Victoria
10959

Found at Departure Bay, near Nanaimo. Waterworn, so that features are partly obliterated. Published in Duff, 1956a, p. 33.

37
Seated Human Figure Bowl

Height: 5"
Provincial Museum, Victoria
6157

Found at Royston, south of Courtenay on Vancouver Island. Published in Duff, 1956a, p. 38, Pl. 13d; also in Wingert, 1952, Pl. 40.

38
Seated Human Figure Bowl

Height: 7½"
Provincial Museum, Victoria
6156

Found during railroad construction on the shore of Comox Harbour south of Courtenay. Soapstone. Published in Duff, 1956a, p. 38, Pl. 12b. The large face on the front of the bowl, with nose punned also as beak, is found on other such bowls, and is reminiscent of the "hawk" of Northwest Coast art.

39
Seated Human Figure Bowl

Height: 4"
Museum of Anthropology, University of B.C.
Personal property of Dr. C. E. Borden
DhRs1:9216

Found on a disturbed surface of the Marpole site, Vancouver, this soapstone figurine is attributed to the Marpole Phase (c. 400 B.C.-A.D. 450) by Borden. References: Duff, 1956a, p. 31, Pl. 13f; Borden, 1970, Fig. 31; Masterpieces, 1969, Pl. 28.

40
Seated Human Figure Bowl

Height: 21½"
Courtesy of the Museum of the American Indian, Heye Foundation, New York.
5/586

Said to be from the Marpole midden, this large image was rediscovered by Hilary Stewart during the survey for this exhibition. It had formerly been known only from a cast in the Provincial Museum, made in 1916. Published in Duff, 1956a, p. 39, Fig. 2, as Martin Bowl No. 1.

41
Seated Human Figure Bowl

Height: 7½"
Courtesy of the Museum of the American Indian, Heye Foundation, New York
1/9485

According to museum records, this complex soapstone image was collected in 1870 in a shellmound, six feet below the surface, Washington.

42
Seated Human Figure Bowl

Height: 13½"
Courtesy of the Museum of the American Indian, Heye Foundation, New York
10/1957

Lummi Island, Puget Sound, Washington

43
Seated Human Figure Bowl

Height: 8"
National Museum of Man, Ottawa
XII-B-1798

Found in the bank of the Alouette River near Haney in the Fraser Valley. Unusually complex in design, with snake and bird heads. Published in Duff, 1956a, p. 30, Pl. 7; Dickason, 1972, Pl. 9. The nose-beaked figure on the front of the bowl is very much like the northern Northwest Coast "hawk", which is now considered a symbol of the state of transformation. (WD)

44
Seated Human Figure Bowl

Height: 8½"
Centennial Museum, Vancouver
QAA-1076

Webster's Corners, near Haney in Fraser Valley.

45
Seated Human Figure Bowl

Height: 9¼"
Centennial Museum, Vancouver
QAA-1077

Found about 1920 two miles from the Fraser River near Webster's Corners, in situation suggesting great age. Snake extends down back. Published in Duff, 1956a, Pl. 5b, p. 29. as Skytte Bowl.

46
**Head of Seated Human
Figure Bowl**

Height: 4″
Mr. James Garrison, Vancouver, B.C.

Found in 1972 in Chilliwack. The head is unusual in the shape of the eyes and in the depiction of hair. The nose, broken off, was large and had a pierced septum. The stone, light soapstone, shows signs of burning. The neck has been sawn or abraded to a flat surface which serves as a base for the head.

47
**Body of Seated Human
Figure Bowl**

Height: 5½″
Museum of Anthropology, University of B.C.
DhR18:43

Found in the 1960s in Chilliwack. The chest as well as head is broken away. Unusual in the explicit depiction of hands and arms but no legs. Shoulder blades, ribs, and (battered) backbone are depicted. Light soapstone. Is it the body of No. 46?

48
**Head of Seated Human
Figure Bowl**

Height: 6″
Museum of Anthropology, University of B.C.
A 1632

Provenience unknown. Published in Duff, 1956a, p. 41, Pl. 14d. This has been called "Brooks head No. 1", and is from the enigmatic Brooks Collection of stone carvings, the place of which in the prehistory of the area is not yet understood. (See Duff, 1956a, p. 90.)

49
**Seated Human
Figure Bowl**

Height: 9¼″
Centennial Museum, Vancouver
QA-350

Published in Duff, 1956a, p. 40 and Pl. 12a as Seward Bowl. Included in this series despite the fact that it was said to be from Alaska.

50
**Seated Human
Figure Bowl**

Height: 8½″
Provincial Museum, Victoria
2996

Found at Ruby Creek, below Hope on the Fraser River. Published in Smith, 1923, Pl. XVIII, Fig. 2; Inverarity, 1950, Pl. 42; Duff, 1956a, p. 27, Fig. 1.

51
**Seated Human
Figure Bowl**

Height: 4¾″
Provincial Museum, Victoria
6899

Found on the west side of the Fraser River across from Lytton, in an ancient disturbed burial. The face strongly resembles the style of the northern Northwest Coast. Published in Duff, 1956a, p. 24, Pl. 2b and Pl. 23.

52
Seated Human Figure Bowl

Height: 5¾"
Provincial Museum, Victoria
EbRj22:1

Found by N. Karholm in 1937 with a disturbed burial across the Fraser River from Lytton. Unique features are the upside-down frog on the front, the perforated bowl, and the upside-down bowl in the base. Published in Duff, 1956a, p. 24, Pl. 3 as the Karholm Bowl.

53
Seated Human Figure Bowl

Height: 3½"
Simon Fraser University Museum of Anthropology and Archaeology.

This fine little sculpture was ploughed up at a house-pit village site at Rattlesnake Flat, on the Fraser near Lytton. The figure on the brow is a rattlesnake, the one on the back is a Northwestern toad. References: Duff, 1956a, p. 25, Pl. 4a as the Copper Kettle bowl of Mr. S. K. Baker; also Baker, 1970, Fig. 10. Date estimate: 500-1000 A.D.

54
Seated Human Figure Bowl

Height: 7¾"
Courtesy of the Museum of the American Indian, Heye Foundation, New York
1847

Lytton. References: Duff, 1956a, p. 23 (the Heye Bowl); Smith, 1907, p. 422 and Pl. 185a; Smith, 1923, Pl. 20-1.

55
Seated Human Figure Bowl

Height: 7"
National Museum of Man, Ottawa
VII-G-620

"Probably from Lytton." The bulgy cheeks of this figure represent snakes. From the Bossom Collection. Published in Duff, 1956a, p. 25, Pl. 13a; also M. W. Smith, 1956, Pl. Ca.

56
Seated Human Figure Bowl

Height: 10"
Centennial Museum, Vancouver
QAD-1692

Found in 1956 on the Fraser River near Lillooet. Incised ribs and backbone. Split snake on front. Published in Duff, 1956a, Pl. 1, p. 41, as the Lillooet Bowl No. 2.

57
Seated Human Figure Bowl

Height: 7¼"
Provincial Museum, Victoria
263

This famous image was found in the Indian burial ground at Kamloops. It has been published in Hill-Tout, 1899, p. 18; Smith, 1900, Fig. 380; Smith, 1913, Pl. XVe; Wingert, 1952, Pl. 41; Duff, 1956a,

p. 23; Masterpieces . . . , Pl. 22.

According to Hill-Tout, this bowl was said by the Indians to have been used in women's puberty ceremonies. The sitting figure is said to represent a woman giving birth to a child. The depression "held the sacred water with which the shaman sprinkled the girl on her return from retirement in the woods". A snake extends down the back.

58
Sawn Nephrite

Length: 12½"
Centennial Museum, Vancouver, B.C.
QA-346

The local "jade" was found by the native people as boulders in the Fraser River, and was sawn and polished into cutting blades. This block is the image of blade-making.

59
Nephrite Blade

Length: 12½"
Centennial Museum, Vancouver, B.C.
QAD-1476

From the upper Fraser Valley. This "larger than life" chisel is best considered as a "property celt", an object of wealth and an image of jade.

60
Bird

Length: 4½"
Centennial Museum, Vancouver, B.C.
QAA-923

Found at Minstrel Island in the Kwakiutl area, this little image may have fitted on the end of a staff, or may have been a spear-thrower weight.

61
Smoking Pipe: Fish

Length: 6"
Courtesy of the Museum of the American Indian, Heye Foundation, New York
20/6184

Found at Lytton, such pipes were smoked in native times with a locally grown species of tobacco. The ancient American custom of smoking did not extend any farther north or west at the time of the arrival of Europeans. The tobacco used by the Haida was chewed rather than smoked, until smoking was adopted by them from the white man.

62
Bear

Height: 3⅛"
Kamloops Museum, Kamloops, B.C.
A-677

Found at the Chase burial site near Kamloops, this little soapstone bear shows red pigment around the eyes and on the arms and legs. Use unknown.

63
Bear

Height: 2"
Kamloops Museum, Kamloops, B.C.
A-678

Found at the Chase burial site near Kamloops, this little soapstone bear shows red pigment around the eyes and on the arms and legs. Use unknown.

64
Eagle

Height: 2¼"
Provincial Museum, Victoria, B.C.
1585

Collected in 1913 by Dr. C. F. Newcombe at Greenville, Nass River, this powerful little sculpture is said to represent an eagle. It has been called a charm, but may have been a staff head. Crevices show red pigment. References: Inverarity, 1950, No. 37; Hawthorn, 1956, Fig. 104.

65
Man

Height: 7½"
National Museum of Man, Ottawa.
XII-B-604

Collected at Metlakatla by I. W. Powell in 1879, this understated figure may have an association with the stone clubs collected at the same time: 108, 110, 111.

66
Phallus-Man

Extent: 6½"
Courtesy of the Museum of the American Indian, Heye Foundation, New York
19-876

Bella Coola, King's Island, collected by Jacobsen. Both a "part" and a whole at the same time, this little pun is both phallus and man.

67
Mother and Child

Height: 5⅜"
Museum of Anthropology, University of B.C., Vancouver
A 1352 (A1112)

Collected at Bella Bella by Dr. G. E. Darby. References: Inverarity, 1950, Fig. 46; Hawthorn, 1956, Fig. 63.

68
"Stone Marker"

Length: 7½"
National Museum of Man, Ottawa.
VII-C-104

Collected by Dr. C. F. Newcombe on the Nass River, this object is catalogued as a "stone marker", but its manner of use is unknown. Perhaps it is nothing more than an expression of relationship, or of measurement.

69
Charm: The Hand-Eye Combination

Height: 1⅝"
National Museum of Man, Ottawa
VII-C-271

Collected by C. F. Newcombe at Gitlakdamiks, Nass River.

70
Hand Hammer

Height: 7"
Museum of Anthropology, University of B.C.
A 1646

The type specimen of the Northwest Coast hand hammer.

71
Pestle

Length: 12"
Museum of Anthropology, University of B.C.
A7239

Bella Coola.

72
Hand Hammer, Nippletop

Height: 8¾"
Langley Centennial Museum, Fort Langley, B.C.
63-3-2

In the Fraser Valley the principal embellishment of the basic handmaul consisted of multiple rings on the nipple top.

73
Hand Hammer (Zoomorphic Maul)

Height: 8½"
Vernon Museum, Archives, and Art Gallery, Vernon, B.C.
40-60-13

From Chase, B.C. Mauls with generalized animal heads are sparsely scattered throughout the province.

74
Hand Maul: Phalliform

Extent: 9¾"
Provincial Museum, Victoria, B.C.
1069

Interior Salish, south Thompson area, collected by C. Hill-Tout in 1898. This is one of a small number of known examples which make the phallic metaphor an explicit phalliform statement.

75
Phalliform Pestle

Extent: 9¼"
Centennial Museum, Vancouver, B.C.
QAA-524

No further data.

76
Hand Hammer:
Man with Hat

Height: 8½"
National Museum of Man, Ottawa
VII-B-908

Haida, Queen Charlotte Islands. Incised areas appear lighter, suggesting the carving was added at a later date.

This is a common type of hand hammer, which is redefined by the image into a little cloaked man with a hat.

77
Pestle: Raven

Length: 9"
Smithsonian Institution, Washington, D.C.
67849

Tlingit, collected at Kootznahoo by J. J. McLean in 1882. "For preparing native tobacco." Illustrated in U.S. National Museum Annual Report for 1888, P1. 63.

78
Hand Hammer
(T-shaped Maul)

Width: 5"
Provincial Museum, Victoria, B.C.
1485

Masset Haida. A type specimen of the T-shaped maul.

79
Hand Hammer
(Stirrup Maul)

Height: 5½"
National Museum of Man, Ottawa
VII-X-988

No data. From Bossom Collection.

80
Hand Hammer
(Stirrup Maul)

Height: 5¼"
Courtesy of the Museum of the American Indian, Heye Foundation, New York
17/5261

B.C. Ends carved to show human faces.

81
Hand Hammer
(Stirrup Maul)

Height: 6½"
Smithsonian Institution, Washington, D.C.
23417

Alaska, collected by J. G. Swan. Combines the conceptual play of both stirrup maul and sloped maul, with the "ends" being different, and one "eating" the other. (WD)

82
Hand Hammer
(Slope-handled Maul)

Height: 9"
Ms. Dolly Jensen, courtesy of the Tongass Historical Society Museum, Ketchikan, Alaska.

The family heirloom of a Tlingit family, this master-piece of slope-handled mauls seems to have been made, not for use, but as a work of pure sculpture. As such, it is the crowning image of the conceptual sequence of hand hammers described in the text. Reference: *Far North*, 1973, Fig. 244.

83
Hand Hammer (Slope-Handled Maul)

Height: 6¼"
Smithsonian Institution, Washington, D.C.
378199

Tlingit. In this sensuous little sculpture, the upper head is mouthed, looking for its missing partner. (WD)

84
Slave Killer

Length: 14"
Provincial Museum, Victoria, B.C.
10855

Kwakiutl, collected at Fort Rupert, 1866-71. Published in Gunther, 1962, Pl. 200; Masterpieces . . . , 1969, No. 116; Dickason, 1972, p. 31.

85
Slave Killer

Length: 10¼"
Centennial Museum, Vancouver, B.C.
QAA-1066
Kwakiutl.

86
Slave Killer

Length: 15"
Centennial Museum, Vancouver, B.C.
QAA-1067

Kwakiutl.

87
Head of Slave Killer

Height: 3¼"
Centennial Museum, Vancouver, B.C.
QAA-519

No data.

88
Head of Slave Killer

Height: 4¾"
Provincial Museum, Victoria
2096

Kwakiutl, Alert Bay.

89
Slave Killer or Club

Length: 14"
Mr. John Hauberg, Seattle, Washington.

This club was collected at Nootka in 1778 by Captain James Cook, and was acquired for the Leverian Museum in London. "In 1783, a young artist named Sarah Stone sketched all of the Cook artifacts in water color. Her Sketch Book vanished but came to light 10 or 15 years ago and was acquired . . . for the Bishop Museum in Honolulu which published them under the title of *Art and Artifacts of the 18th Century . . .* in 1968." (John Hauberg, personal communication, December 18, 1974.

90
Hafted Hammer: The "Hawk" that Eats Whales

Length: 8"
National Museum of Man, Ottawa
VII-B-924

Haida, Skidegate, collected by I. W. Powell in 1879. This is the masterpiece of hafted mauls, adapting to the maul the image of "Skiamsum" or "Thunderbird" with a whale in its mouth (WD).

91
Hafted Hammer Head: Animal Head

Length: 5¼"
National Museum of Man, Ottawa
VII-C-82

Grooved maul collected at Fort Rupert in 1879 by I. W. Powell.

92
Hafted Hammer Head: Animal Head

Length: 12"
Provincial Museum, Victoria
12635

Grooved maul from old Hartley Bay (Tsimshian).

93
Hafted Hammer Head: Animal Head

Length: 7¼"
Mr. Barry Roome,
Shawnigan Lake, B.C.

Haida, Queen Charlotte Islands

94
Hafted Hammer Head: Animal Head

Length: 5"
National Museum of Man, Ottawa
VII-B-1067

Haida

95
Hafted Hammer Head: Animal Head

Length: 6¼"
National Museum of Man, Ottawa
VII-B-922

Haida perforated maul, collected from Queen Charlotte Islands by I. W. Powell in 1879.

96
Hafted Hammer: Raven Alighting

Length: 6¼"
Mr. W. R. Quanstrom, Terrace, B.C.

Found at Lakelse Lake by a fire-fighting crew. Represents Raven alighting or taking off, punned onto the structure of the usual image, a head.

97
Pile Driver:
Dogfish Head

Length: 15½"
Louise and Walter Arensberg Collection, Philadelphia Museum of Art, Philadelphia.
50-134-483

Kwakiutl. In use, the thumbs fit into the "eyes", and grooves on the opposite side accommodate the fingers. The striking surface is the back of the head. This is the crowning image of the pile driver, and has been widely published (Inverarity, 1950, Pl. 52; Covarrubias, 1954, Fig. 59; Wardwell, 1964, Pl. 186.) It is here interpreted (WD) as the Dogfish or Shark, which was among the list of family crests, but seems to have had an additional structural meaning, in combining a "head" of phallic outline with a fearsome "mouth".

98
Pile Driver:
Circular Face

Diameter: 12¾"
Provincial Museum, Victoria
6507

Kwakiutl, Rivers Inlet.

99
Pile Driver

Length: 10½"
Museum of Anthropology, University of B.C.
A6438
Nass River Tsimshian, prehistoric.

100
Pile Driver

Diameter: 11"
Courtesy of the Museum of the American Indian, Heye Foundation, New York
2/8503

Kwakiutl, collected by George Hunt. Here interpreted (WD) as a head in the hands, tongue hanging out, suggesting a headache from all that pounding.

101
Stone Club

Length: 13½"
Courtesy of the Museum of the American Indian, Heye Foundation, New York
5/5059

Club from Hagwilget cache; phallic handle, mouthed image at other end, and half-circle arch joining the two. Published in Duff, 1963, Fig. 1c, p. 5; Dockstader, 1962, Pl. 1. See note on No. 104 for museum documentation.

102
Stone Club

Length: 13⅞"
Provincial Museum, Victoria
9548

Sandstone, representing sandhill crane. This is one of about 35 clubs found together in a cache at Hagwilget on the Bulkley River in 1898 (see Duff, 1962). Also published in Masterpieces . . . , 1969, Pl. 23.

103
Stone Club

Length: 12½"
Courtesy of the Museum of the American Indian,

Heye Foundation, New York
5/5058

Club from Hagwilget cache. One end phallic, the other has a bird-like head which resembles a surf scoter. Published in Duff, 1962, No. 32.

104
Stone Club:
Bi-phallic

Length: 18½"
Courtesy of the Museum of the American Indian,
Heye Foundation, New York
5/5057

According to C. F. Newcombe and W.D., this club is from the Hagwilget cache. Museum records say: "Found with 5/5058 and 5/5059 in rock cave on site of old Niska Valley. Buckley Canyon. Collector, Emmons. Traces of red pigment at the top."

105
Stone Club:
Death-Bringer

Length: 18"
Courtesy of the Museum of the American Indian,
Heye Foundation, New York.
12/3273

This masterpiece among clubs has the diamond-shaped blade of many of the clubs found in the Hagwilget cache, and a strange human head on the handle which might be interpreted as representing death. According to the museum records, it was found on the same site as the cache ("Spring, 1922, under two-foot cedar stump near Two-Mile Creek; old Gitksan village site, Bulkley Canyon, 4 miles from Hazelton.") References: Dockstader, 1962, Pl. 4; Duff, 1963, p. 7 and Fig. 3a.

106
Stone Club

Length: 12"
Provincial Museum, Victoria
4855

This object from the Hazelton area is identified as a club on the basis of its similarities to the others, notably the phallic handle. The sculpturing on the main body, though incomplete, defies ordinary identification. If this club is an equation, one can say no more than that the one end is a form of order, the other a form of chaos. Published in Duff, 1963. p. 7 and Fig. 3c.

107
Stone Club

Length: 18"
Centennial Museum, Vancouver, B.C.
QAA-1070

Kitimat. Said to represent kingfisher. Phallic handle. This club could be seen as a self-swallowing Raven. (WD)

108
Stone Club

Length: 8¾"
National Museum of Man, Ottawa
XII-B-560

From Metlakatla, collected by I. W. Powell in 1879. Published in Duff, 1963 (p. 9, Fig. 4e) where it is identified as a fish.

109
Stone Club

Length: 10"
National Museum of Man, Ottawa
VII-X-427

No data. Resembles No. 108, which has been identified as a fish, but which can equally be seen as a self-swallowing mouth, as can Nos. 106 and 101.

110
Stone Club

Length: 8¾"
National Museum of Man, Ottawa
XII-B-559

Collected at Metlakatla in 1879 by I. W. Powell. The strange human head evokes memories of the masterful No. 105 from Hazelton. It is one of several clubs from Metlakatla which seem to be pale shadows of the Hagwilget forms. Published in Duff, 1963, Fig. 4j, p. 9.

111
Stone Club

Length: 15"
National Museum of Man, Ottawa
XII-B-556

Collected at Metlakatla in 1879 by I. W. Powell. This is another club which seems to be conceptually derivative of a type from Hagwilget, but technically inferior. Published in Duff, 1963, Fig. 4b, p. 8.

112
Stone Club

Length: 10"
Centennial Museum, Vancouver, B.C.
QAA-1072

Found on Quadra Island.

113
Stone Club

Length: 12½"
Provincial Museum, Victoria
4043

Found 3 miles south of Powell River in 1923.

114
Stone Club

Length: 13"
Provincial Museum, Victoria
752

Found on the north arm of Burrard Inlet in 1894. Such clubs with projecting axe-like blades are more common in Oregon and California, where they are called "slave-killers" (see Duff, 1956a, p. 87; Duff, 1963).

115
Paint Dish

Length: 8½"
Centennial Museum, Vancouver, B.C.
QAA-108

Kwakiutl, Quatsino Sound. The open side is a face, the bottom a body with arms and legs. The bowl is therefore a mouth and a belly at the same time (WD).

116
Paint Dish: Frog

Length: 6"
McCord Museum, McGill University, Montreal
1206

Haida, collected at Skidegate by George M. Dawson in 1878. Reference: Dawson, 1880, Pl. VIII, No. 12.

117
Bowl or Paint Dish

Length: 9½"
Smithsonian Institution, Washington, D.C.
89022

Haida (Skidegate), purchased by J. G. Swan, 1883, for $1.00. Incised design.

118
Bowl: Animal-form

Length: 5¾"
National Museum of Man, Ottawa
XII-B-322

Kwakiutl, collected at Fort Rupert by I. W. Powell in 1879.

119
Tobacco Mortar: Beaver

Length: 9½"
Mr. and Mrs. R. E. B. Gore-Langton, Victoria, B.C.

Haida, from Masset. Behind the beaver's face are human hands, and on the beaver's tail is a human mask. Shown in the Arts of the Raven show, No. 425.

120
Tobacco Mortar: Beaver

Length: 9½"
National Museum of Man, Ottawa
XII-B-318

Haida, collected from the Queen Charlotte Islands by I. W. Powell in 1879. Reference: Smith, 1923, Pls. IV and V (line drawings).

121
Tobacco Mortar: Frog and Man

Length: 5"
McCord Museum, McGill University, Montreal, P.Q.
1205 c

Haida.

122
Tobacco Mortar: Frog with Eyebrows

Length: 10½"
Smithsonian Institution, Washington, D.C.
75401

Collected at Sitka, Alaska, in 1884 by John J. McLean.

123
Tobacco Mortar: Frog

Length: 9"
McCord Museum, McGill University, Montreal
1205b

Haida, collected by George M. Dawson in 1878. Reference: Dawson, 1880 Pl. VIII, No. 15.

124
Tobacco Mortar: Frog

Length: 9"
National Museum of Man, Ottawa
XII-B-317

Haida. Collected in 1879 by I. W. Powell. Published (line drawings) in Smith, 1923, Pls. V and VI.

125
Tobacco Mortar: Frog

Length: 5½"
Courtesy of the Museum of the American Indian, Heye Foundation, New York
4/420

Haida.

126
Mortar: Emerging Frog and "Hawk"

Length: 6"
National Museum of Man, Ottawa
VII-B-836

Haida, from Skidegate, collected by Aaronson.

127
Tobacco Mortar: Frog, Seal, and Human

Length: 17"
McCord Museum, McGill University, Montreal
1205a

Haida, collected from Kiusta (according to *Master-*

pieces catalogue) by George M. Dawson in 1878. References: Dawson, 1880, Pl. VIII, No. 11; *Masterpieces*, 1969, Pl. 85. Here interpreted as Frog crest of Edenshaw, chief of Kiusta.

128
Tobacco Mortar: Grinning Bear

Length: 11½"
Smithsonian Institution, Washington, D.C.
221181

Collected by G. T. Emmons. Acquired 1903. Tlingit (Killisnoo). "Of marble, held a long time in the Tagwayta family of the Hootz-ah-tai-gwan through many generations of chiefs." Published in Harner and Elsasser, 1965; *Far North*, 1972, Pl. 241.

129
Tobacco Mortar: Bear

Length: 13¼"
Museum of Northern B.C., Prince Rupert
2219

The image has not fully emerged from the stone, and is ambiguous: bear or frog? A second face is beginning to emerge from the other end.

130
Tobacco Mortar: Seal

Length: 10"
Smithsonian Institution, Washington, D.C.
45961

Collected at Sitka, Alaska, in 1881 by John J. McLean. Used for grinding native tobacco for chewing. Published in U.S. National Museum Annual Report, 1888, Pl. 63.

131
Tobacco Mortar: Raven

Length: 12½"
Provincial Museum, Victoria
4115

From an early collection. Catalogued as Haida, and as representing a diver (loon). Published in Inverarity, 1950; People of the Potlatch, 1956; Arts of the Raven, 1967, No. 426; Masterpieces . . . , 1969, Pl. 84.

132
Tobacco Mortar: Raven

Length: 12"
Courtesy of the Museum of the American Indian, Heye Foundation, New York
11/5854

Tsimshian, Port Simpson, B.C. Collected by Emmons. Here interpreted as a threshold pun, hinting at Raven but with faint echoes of frog and bear. (WD)

133
Tobacco Mortar: Mouth

Length: 9"
National Museum of Man, Ottawa
XII-B-315

Haida, collected by C. F. Newcombe from Klue.

134
Tobacco Mortar: One Human Face, Four Times

Diameter: 12½"
Smithsonian Institution, Washington, D.C.
220185

From Skeena River, B.C. Purchased in Victoria by G. T. Emmons. Accessioned 1903. Published in Feder, 1971; Far North, 1972.

135
Mask

Diameter: 9"
National Museum of Man, Ottawa
VII-C-329

Basalt, collected at Kitkatla, a coastal Tsimshian village, in 1879 by Indian Commissioner I. W. Powell. Published in Gunther, 1962, p. 25, Pl. 128; Harner and Elsasser, 1965, p. 108; Masterpieces . . . , 1969, Pl. 53.; Dickason, 1972, Pl. 17.

136
Mask

Diameter: 9"
Musée de l'Homme, Paris
81.22.1

The following is a translation of the caption published in Chefs-d-OEuvre du Musee de l'Homme, Musée de l'Homme, Paris, 1965, p. 160, Pl.54: "Mask in hard greenish stone, representing a human face. The outside and the periphery are very carefully polished; the eyes, not drawn, are simple holes, and two large flat bands have been left intentionally rough to represent eyebrows. The lips, the ears, and the eyebrows carry traces of red paint. A series of very regular perforations, made by a drill, allow the attachment of the mask to the face. In spite of its considerable weight (4.17 kg.), it was made to be worn, attached by straps or thongs, the wearer gripping between his teeth a loop of willow attached by two holes in the base. Hamy, who studied this piece in 1897, is said to have seen this loop still in place: "This handle, or loop of willow . . . has been used often enough to carry the exact imprints of the wearer's teeth." The use of these masks is general in North America. The Indians of the Northwest Coast believed in the existence of spirits that often had evil power. Through his mask, the initiate obtained help from these supernatural beings or became one himself. The style of this piece is similar to the wooden masks of the Tlingit Indians of Sitka. Donated by Alphonse Pinart, No. 81.22.1."

bibliography

BARBEAU, Marius 1953 *Haida Myths Illustrated in Argillite Carvings.* Ottawa, National Museum of Canada.

BOAS, F. 1890 The Shuswap. *Sixth Report on the Northwestern Tribes of Canada.* British Association for the Advancement of Science.

BORDEN, Charles E. 1970 Culture History of the Fraser Delta Region: an Outline. In Carlson, R. L. (ed.) Archaeology in British Columbia, New Discoveries. *B.C. Studies* (Special Issue), Vancouver.

CALKOWSKI, Marcia 1974 Cannibalism and Infertility among the Thompson, Lillooet, and Shuswap: The Shaman as Sexual Mediator. Master of Arts Thesis (Anthropology), University of British Columbia.

COVARRUBIAS, Miguel 1954 *The Eagle, the Jaguar and the Serpent: Indian Art of the Americas.* New York.

DAWSON, George M. 1880 "On the Haida Indians of the Queen Charlotte Islands." Appendix A: *Report on the Queen Charlotte Islands.* Montreal: Dawson.

DICKASON, Olive P. 1972 *Indian Arts in Canada.* Department of Indian Affairs and Northern Development, Ottawa, Canada.

DOCKSTADER, Frederick J. 1961 *Indian Art in America.* New York Graphic Society.

DUFF, W. 1956a Prehistoric Stone Sculpture of the Fraser River and Gulf of Georgia. *Anthropology in British Columbia*, No. 5. Provincial Museum, Victoria, B.C.

DUFF, W. 1956b Unique Stone Artifacts from the Gulf Islands. Provincial Museum Annual Report for 1955, pp. 45-55. Victoria, B.C.

DUFF, W. 1963 Stone Clubs from the Skeena River Area, Provincial Museum Annual Report for 1962, pp. 2-12. Victoria, B.C.

DUFF, W., with Bill Holm and Bill Reid 1967 *Arts of the Raven.* The Vancouver Art Gallery, Vancouver, B.C.

FEDER, Norman 1971 *Two Hundred Years of North American Indian Art.* Whitney Museum of Art. New York

FOSTER, Mrs. W. G. 1926 Stone Images and Implements, and Some Petroglyphs. *Museum Notes*, Vol. 1, No. 3. Vancouver Art, Historical, and Scientific Association, Vancouver, B.C.

GUNTHER, Erna   1962   *Northwest Coast Indian Art.* An Exhibit at the Seattle World's Fair.

HARNER, Michael J. and A.B. Elsasser   1965   *Art of the Northwest Coast.* An Exhibition at the Lowie Museum of Anthropology, Berkeley, California.

HAWTHORN, Audrey E.   1956   *People of the Potlatch.* Vancouver Art Gallery and University of B.C., Vancouver.

HAWTHORN, Audrey E.   1967   *Art of the Kwakiutl Indians and Other Northwest Coast Tribes.* University of British Columbia and University of Washington Press.

HILL-TOUT, C.   1899   Notes of the Prehistoric Races of British Columbia and their Monuments. *British Columbia Mining Record.*

HILL-TOUT, C.   1928   *The Great Fraser Midden.* Vancouver Art, Historical, and Scientific Association, Vancouver, B.C.

INVERARITY, R. B.   1950   *Art of the Northwest Coast Indians.* University of California Press.

LEISK, H.   1934   Archaeology in Vancouver. *Vancouver Sun,* September 8, 1934, p. 6.

LEISK, H.   n.d.   Field Notes in Vancouver Centennial Museum.

MITCHELL, Donald H.   1972   Archaeology of the Gulf of Georgia Area, a Natural Region and Its Culture Types. *Syesis,* Volume 4, Supplement 1. Provincial Museum, Victoria.

National Gallery of Art, Washington   1973   *The Far North: 2000 Years of American Eskimo and Indian Art.*

SIEBERT, Erna and Werner Forman   1967   *North American Indian Art.* Paul Hamlyn, Ltd.

SMITH, Harlan I.   1907   Archaeology of the Gulf of Georgia and Puget Sound. *American Museum of Natural History,* Memoirs, Vol. 4, No. 6.

SMITH, Harlan I.   1923   *An Album of Prehistoric Canadian Art.* Canada, Department of Mines Bulletin No. 37, Anthropological Series No. 8. Ottawa

Societe des Amis du Musee de l'Homme   1969   *Masterpieces of Indian and Eskimo Art from Canada.* Paris.

STEWART, Hilary   1973   *Artifacts of the Northwest Coast Indians.* Hancock House Publishers, Saanichton, B.C.

STURTEVANT, W.C. (compiler)   1973   *Boxes and Bowls:* Decorated Containers by Nineteenth-Century Haida, Tlingit, Bella Bella, and Tsimshian Indian Artists. Published for the Renwick Gallery of the National Collection of Fine Arts by the Smithsonian Institution Press. Washington.

TEIT, James A.   1900   The Thompson Indians. *Publications of the Jesup North Pacific Expedition,* Vol. I, Part IV, ed. Franz

		Boas. Memoirs of the American Museum of Natural History, Vol. II. Leiden: E. J. Brill.
TEIT, James A.	1912	"The Mythology of the Thompson Indians." *Publications of the Jesup North Pacific Expedition,* Vol. VIII, Part II, ed. by Franz Boas. Memoirs of the American Museum of Natural History, Vol. XII. Leiden. E. J. Brill.
WARDWELL, Allen	1964	*Yakutat South, Indian Art of the Northwest Coast.* Art Institute of Chicago.
WINGERT, Paul S.	1952	*Prehistoric Stone Sculpture of the Pacific Northwest.* Portland Art Museum.